# Jesus
## God by Nature

by

Constantine D. Lenis

*To Pastor Ken Russell with Christian love. "Gus"*

**DORRANCE PUBLISHING CO., INC.**
**PITTSBURGH, PENNSYLVANIA 15222**

ISBN # 0-8059-3954-7
Printed in the United States of America

*First Printing*

For information or to order additional books, please write:
Dorrance Publishing Co., Inc.
643 Smithfield Street
Pittsburgh, Pennsylvania 15222
U.S.A.

# COLOSSIANS 1:16 according to the:

## Greek Text

"ΕΝ ΑΥΤΩ ΕΚΤΙΣΘΗ ΤΑ ΠΑΝΤΑ, . . . ΤΑ
In (within) Him were created the all things . . . the

ΠΑΝΤΑ ΔΙ' ΑΥΤΟΥ ΚΑΙ ΕΙΣ ΑΥΤΟΝ ΕΚΤΙΣΤΑΙ."
all things by Him and to Him were created

## Author's Translation of the above Text
"In Him (i.e. within Him) all things were created
. . . all things were created by Him and for Him."

## The Interlinear Bible (J. P. Green, Sr.)
"for all things were created in Him, ... all things
have been created through Him, and for Him."

## Jehovah's Witnesses' translation ( NWT )
"Because by means of him all [other]* things
were created . . . All [other]* things have been
created through him and for him."

---

* The word "other" is not found in the Greek text. This
word was inserted in parenthesis by the Witnesses to
support their theory that Jesus is a created being.

## The author's explanation of the above text is found on pp. 124 - 127.

# TABLE OF CONTENTS

# TABLE OF CONTENTS --- Continued

*For Your Glory, Lord.*

Formerly, when you did not know God, you were slaves to those who by nature are not gods.

Apostle Paul (NIV)

# PROLOGUE

Dear Reader,

For many years I tried to find the truth and the meaning of life. There were many things I thought were true which, after careful investigation, were proven useless and untrue.

Although I met people in various groups who seemed to be totally satisfied, I, in my quest to find continuous joy and satisfaction, was unsuccessful. My inner self was empty because, for many years, I did not know Him who fills all things. (Eph. 4 : 10)

My joy started to increase from the time <u>He was revealed to me</u>. Since then, I have learned that nothing is more precious in life than "the excellency of the knowledge of Christ Jesus, my Lord." (Phil. 3:8)

The apostle Peter, encourages us to "<u>... grow ... in the knowledge of our Lord and Saviour Jesus Christ</u>." (2 Peter 3:18)

The Lord Jesus himself said that the knowledge of God and of Christ is eternal life. (John 17:3) He also said, "... no one knows the Son except the Father, nor does anyone know the Father, except the Son, and he

1.

to whom the Son wills to reveal Him." (Matt. 11:27) Again, He said, "No one is able to come to Me unless the Father ... draws him;" and "... everyone who hears and learns from the Father comes to Me;"
(John 6:44, 45)

From the above words we clearly see that for someone to fully understand Jesus, is not an easy thing. We see that only the Father knows the Son; that only the Son knows the Father; that the Son reveals the Father to whom He wills; that the Father draws the persons to the Son, and whoever hears and learns from the Father comes to the Son, while in another place He says, "... No one comes to the Father except through Me." (John 14:6) What a mystery ! !

Then we hear Jesus saying, "If you had known Me, you would have known My Father also; and from now on you do know Him, and have seen Him."
(John 14:7)

When Jesus said this, Philip, one of His disciples, said to Him, "Lord, show us the Father, and it is enough for us." Jesus said to him, "Am I so long a time with you and you have not known me, Philip? The one seeing Me has seen the Father ! And how do you say show us the Father? Do you not believe that

I am in the Father and the Father is in Me?" (John 14:8-11)

How is it possible for the limited and imperfect human mind to fully understand the vastness and the unlimited nature of God? How can I give examples, based on our limited materialistic world, to try to explain the unlimited nature of the uncreated Godhead? All the examples I use in this book are inadequate and cannot express the divine.

How is it possible for the Son to "dwell", to be "in the Father", and for the Father to "dwell", to be "in the Son", as Jesus said?  What is the <u>nature</u> of Jesus? In order for Him to "dwell" or to be "in the Father", then certainly <u>His nature must be identical to God's</u>.

*If the substance and the nature of the Son were any lower than the substance and the nature of the Father, it would not have endured the co-existence ! He, "the only begotten Son, who is in the bosom of the Father", should be of the same substance and nature as the Father; otherwise if the nature of the Son were different and lower than the nature of the Father, the nature of the Father would have destroyed Him. The same is true even with our own human nature; if a foreign organism invades our body, our body will attack and try to destroy it.*

A man cannot see God and live. (Exod. 33:20) A man, who is a created being, cannot endure such an experience. If Jesus is a created being, how can He endure seeing God, and have all the fullness of the Godhead dwelling in Him bodily? (Col. 2:9)

> Thus, the fact that all the fullness of the "Diety by nature" dwells in Him bodily, proves that Jesus is God by nature !

All those who saw Jesus when He was on earth, saw the "God by nature", who had lowered Himself by becoming flesh and revealed to us His glory in the face of Jesus Christ ! (1 Tim. 3:16; 2 Cor. 4:6)

If you, beloved reader, have reached the point in your life where you are searching the Scriptures trying to understand our Lord Jesus, you are doing well. I did the same. Your personal searching of the Scriptures and the revelation by the Holy Spirit will help you to come to know Him. To those who were searching the Scriptures during His time on earth, Jesus said, " ... they (the Scriptures) are the ones witnessing about Me." (John 5:39)

The knowledge of the mystery of God and of Christ, is the most excellent thing in the life of a Christian.

The apostle Paul was encouraging his Christian brothers to come to this knowledge when he wrote, "that their hearts may be comforted, being joined together in love, and to all riches of the full assurance of the understanding, to the full knowledge of the mystery of God, even of the Father and of Christ*, in whom are hidden all the treasures of wisdom and of knowledge." (Col. 2:2,3)

With great joy, I present to you my personal search of the Scriptures on the subject of the "Nature of Christ", which began with a revelation by the Holy Spirit to me and which was enriched by the input of many men of God.

I hope that some of the points I raise here, will help you to grow in the "... knowledge of our Lord and Saviour, Jesus Christ. To Him be the glory, both now and to the day of eternity. Amen." (2 Peter 3:18)

---

* It is worth noting that according to the Greek text of NESTLE-ALAND, the above sentence appears as: "ΤΟΥ ΜΥΣΤΗΡΙΟΥ ΤΟΥ ΘΕΟΥ, ΧΡΙΣΤΟΥ" (OF THE MYSTERY OF THE GOD, CHRIST.) ! !

# CHAPTER ONE

# GOD BY NATURE

**Galatians 4 : 8**    *"But then, indeed not knowing God, you served as slaves to the ones not by nature being gods."*
                      ( from the Greek text )

Men are religious beings. From ancient times to this day, they have made and are still making countless "gods" for themselves. These "gods", whether they are objects or beings who imposed themselves as "gods", whether visible or invisible, like the Olympian gods of the ancient Greeks, the gods of the ancient Egyptians, Mayas, Incas, and others, <u>are not gods by nature,</u> because there is only One who is the true God by nature --- the Creator of all, the fountain of life !

In 1 Corinthians, chapter 8 and verses 5 and 6, the apostle Paul wrote the following:

"For even if some are called gods, either in Heaven or on the earth; even as there are many gods, and many lords; but to us is one God, the Father, of whom are all things, and we for Him; and one Lord Jesus Christ through whom are all things and we by Him".

One of these so-called "gods" is Satan, "the god of this age." (2 Cor. 4:4) His nature is not that of the uncreated God, but that of a created angel; he was a cherub.

When God spoke to the prophet Ezekiel about the King of Tyre, most likely He spoke to the real ruler of Tyre, Satan, to whom all the kingdoms of the earth belong. (Matt. 4:8,9; Luke 4:6)

In Ezekiel chapter 28, verses 11-19, God said to the King of Tyre, "... You have been in Eden, the garden of God; ... You were the anointed cherub that covers, and I had put you ... where you were ... You were perfect in your ways from <u>the day you were created</u>, until iniquity was found in you ... so I cast you profaned from the height (mountain) of God and I destroyed you, O covering cherub ..."

From the above words (verse 15), we see that <u>this cherub was "created". Therefore, as a creature, he is a part of the creation of God. Thus, his nature is not divine. He is not the true God - He is not God by nature.</u>

Only one is the true God by nature -- the eternal God, who has no beginning nor end of days. Satan, on the contrary, had a beginning of days --- the day he was created by God.

Is the Lord Jesus Christ truly God? Is the Son, God by nature? Or is He one of the many so-called gods? Is He a part of God's creation? Is He perhaps a created being? What was His nature from the beginning? What does the Bible say about Him?

In the first chapter of the gospel of John, verse one, we read the following about Him as the "Word" of God:

**"In the beginning was the Word, and the Word was with God, and <u>the Word was God</u>."**

Here, we clearly see that the "Word" was God. In the Greek, the word for God is "ΘΕΟΣ". This word appears twice in this verse. Certain translators of the Bible correctly translated the first appearance of the word as "God"; but, incorrectly translated the second appearance as "DIVINE". They present this verse as follows:

"In the beginning was the Word,  and the Word

was with God, and the Word was DIVINE."

The Greek word for "divine" is "ΘΕΙΟΣ". This word means "a person who comes from God or comes out of God or is sent by God or is protected by God". (Check ΛΕΞΙΚΟΝ ΔΗΜΗΤΡΑΚΟΥ "1970" page 677 under the word "ΘΕΙΟΣ".)

John DID NOT USE the word "ΘΕΙΟΣ" to describe the "Word", but the word "ΘΕΟΣ". He wrote, "the Word was God".

Others, like Jehovah's Witnesses, have added the article "a" before the second word God, in their own translation of the Bible, and they present it like this:

**"In [the] beginning was the Word and the Word was with God and the Word was a god."**

With the expression "a god", they mean that the Word was "another" -- a lesser god than God. Their explanation for this change is that the article "o" (the) is absent before the second word "god"; therefore, they say, since the original Greek text does not read "... and the Word was 'the' God", then that makes the Word to be "a god" -- another god, inferior to the

Father.\* However, if John had written that the Word was "the God", then not only would it have been illogical, because he would have meant that "the God" was from the beginning with "the God", "with or near Himself", but it would also have been unscriptural to say that the Word was God the Father, since the Word is God the Son ! John shows us here what the nature of the Word was: "and the Word was God" -- THAT MEANS WHAT IT SAYS ! From the beginning, the Word did not have the nature or the form of angels, but truly the nature of God ! (For more details about the expression "a god" see Appendix D, page 186.)

In the first chapter of John, verse 18, we read: "No one has seen God at any time; <u>the only-begotten Son,</u> who is in the bosom of the Father, He reveals Him." Therefore, since He is <u>the only-begotten Son (or the only born Son)</u>, and since He came out of the

---

\* In John 4:24, the Greek text reads, "God is Spirit". Here we notice that the article "the" is not found before the word "Spirit". It does not read, "God is the Spirit". The same has been translated into English as, "God is a Spirit". The article "a" here, does not denote that God is one of the many "lesser" created spirits with small "s" ! It simply shows that God is spirit --- not flesh. To make a big issue about the article "a" is very hypocritical of the J.W.'s especially as they are not consistent. In John 1:1, the Greek text reads, "In beginning was the Word". The article "the" is not found before the word "beginning".Yet, in the NWT, they have inserted in brackets the article [the] --- not "a" !

Father, He is at once God by nature, because only God can come out of God, as human can come out of a human, and as only light can come out of light ! (About the "light", compare 1 John 1:5; John 1:9; 3:19) Therefore, the Son is light out of light and true God out of true God !

The apostle Paul wrote the following about the pre-existing Jesus: "... <u>who subsisting in the form of God</u> thought it not robbery to be equal with God, but emptied Himself, taking the form of a slave, having become in the likeness of men and being found in fashion as a man, He humbled Himself ..." (Phil.2:5-8)

> From the above, we see that the form and nature of the pre-human Jesus was that of the uncreated God --- not that of a created angel !

This is why He did not think that it would constitute robbery to be equal with God. And when He emptied Himself, in order to take another form, <u>He did not take the form of angels, but He took an even lower form than theirs and became a man</u>.

One of the big mistakes made by the Jehovah's Witnesses is that they use the words which Jesus spoke <u>as a man</u> and they degrade Him by claiming that He is a lesser god <u>in power, age and knowledge</u> than the Father. They say that the Father is <u>the only true</u>

<u>God</u>. Because of this claim, they are forced to present Jesus as one of the many false gods which are created and are not gods by nature !

In order to support their doctrine, they quote words which <u>the man Jesus</u> said about Himself, like:

"... My Father is greater than I."   (John 14:28)

"I ... go to My Father and your Father, and my God, and your God."   (John 20 : 17)

"But concerning that day and the hour, no one knows, not the angels, those in Heaven, nor the Son, except the Father."   (Mark 13:32)

They also quote the words of the apostle Paul who said about <u>the Christ</u>: "But I want you to know that Christ is the head of every man, and the  man is the head of  a woman, and God is the head of Christ." (1 Cor. 11: 3), and many similar expressions, which prove, as they think, a "hierarchy" !

By saying the above, the Jehovah's Witnesses want to prove that Jesus is not the Father, and that the Father is superior to the Son. (Check their publication: "Should You Believe in the Trinity? --- Is Jesus Christ the Almighty God?").

In their attempt to prove the foregoing, they make a BIG mistake by saying that the "Word", Jesus, is not One of the true Divinity YHWH\*, fully God and God by nature, and they portray Jesus to be a creature ! !

I wonder how they can believe in a God who did not have the ability to speak from the beginning of His existence until the day He decided to "create a creature" which He named His "Word" ! Their theology does not make any sense. God created ALL things by His "Word". If the "Word" is a created being, how did God create the "Word" without the "Word"?

## *The Holy Spirit*

The Witnesses have made a similar mistake with the Spirit of God. They try to strip Him from His living and life-giving personality, and they say that "<u>it is</u>", simply, "<u>the active force</u>" of God, something like the electricity or the radio waves, which are without personality, will, and logic. They try to separate God from His living Word and Spirit !

---

\* YHWH: the Hebrew sacred name for God, the so-called tetragrammaton. "Jehovah" is the modern transliteration of YHWH; the vowels appear through arbitrary transference of the vowel points of "adonai", my Lord. (Webster's New World Dictionary, 1966, page 784, under "Jehovah".)

I wonder how they can believe in a God whose Spirit is an impersonal force, without will and without logic! If their god does not have a Living Spirit, I wonder how he can be alive ! A god made of stone does not have a living spirit !

I am astonished that they believe that the Spirit of God does not have a personality, when they read Scriptures such as the following:

"And while they were doing service to the Lord, and fasting, the Holy Spirit said, . . . separate both Barnabas and Saul to Me, for the work to which I have called them."   (Acts 13 : 2)

The words "to Me"  and "I have called them" show that the Holy Spirit has a personality - is a person.

I am astounded that they believe the Holy Spirit does not have a will, when they read   1 Corinthians 12 : 11:

"But the one and the same Spirit works all these things, distributing separately as He wills." !

These words reveal that the Holy Spirit has a will !

I am astonished that they believe the Holy Spirit is simply an "active force" without logic, when the Bible contains scriptures such as the following:

"For it seemed good to the Holy Spirit and to us ..." (Acts 15 : 28)

"but the Comforter, the Holy Spirit ... He shall teach you all things, and shall remind you of all things that I said to you." (John 14 : 26)

"But when that One comes, the Spirit of truth, He will guide you into all truth;"
(John 16 : 13)

"He, (the Spirit of truth), will announce the coming things to you. He will glorify Me ..."
(John 16 : 13,14)

"And likewise the Spirit also joins in to help our weakness. For we do not know what we should pray for as we ought, but the Spirit Himself pleads our case for us with groanings that cannot be uttered. But the One searching the hearts knows what is the mind of the Spirit, because He intercedes for the saints according to God". (Romans 8 : 26, 27)

"... for the Spirit searches all things, even the deep things of God ... so also no one has known the things of God except the Spirit of God." (1 Cor. 2 : 10, 11)

From the above Scriptures it is plain, that since the Spirit can "teach", "remind", "guide", "announce the coming things", and "glorifies", "helps", "pleads our case", "searches all things" and "knows the things of God", the Spirit must have personality and logic ! !

## A "Hierarchy" ?

We can see, therefore, that Jehovah's Witnesses have not understood the Godhead at all. They are ignoring that the Word and the Spirit of God are LIVING AND ACTIVE, with the full personality of the One and only true God. (Heb. 4 : 12, 13; Romans 8 : 2, 6; 1 Peter 3 : 18; Job 33 : 4; Acts 5 : 3, 4)

---

A man's word is the outer expression of his inner thinking. How foolish it would be to even suggest that the man's word is another being ! How can the Word of God, which is the outer expression of God's inner thought, be another created being totally unrelated to God, as the Witnesses claim?

The fact that the "Word" is not the person of the Godhead who is called the "Father", is beyond any doubt, because the "Word" is the "Son". Certainly, there are differences in the order between the "Father", the "Son "and the "Holy Spirit", observing it from a human viewpoint. For example:

a) the Son did not send the Father to the earth,

b) the Father did not come out of the Son,

c) the Father does not come out of the Holy Spirit,

d) the Holy Spirit did not die on the cross, etc.

God, the Lord of hosts, created everything by His Word and by His Spirit. The Psalmist agrees with this fact because he wrote: **"Through Jehovah's word the heavens were made; and all their hosts by the breath of His mouth."** (Psalm 33 : 6; also read and compare Job 33 : 4 and John 1 : 1-3)

When the "Word" of God became flesh, He lived as a man, whose likeness He took ---- not as God. (John 1 : 14; Phil. 2 : 7, 8)

<u>As a man</u> He said: "... My Father is greater than I." (John 14: 28)

<u>As a man</u> He said: "I am ascending to My Father and your Father, and My God and your God." (John 20:17)

<u>As a man</u> He did not know the day and the hour of the end. (Matthew 24 : 36).

<u>As a man</u> He entrusted everything into the hands of His Heavenly Father, even His own Spirit at the time of His death on the cross. (Luke 23 : 46)

The "hierarchy" which the Witnesses refer to, does not exist in the Godhead. The Bible does not say that such a "hierarchy" exists between the persons of the Godhead. For instance, nowhere does the Bible say that the "head" of the Holy Spirit is the "Word" and that the "head" of the "Word" is the Father ! The word "hierarchy" does not even exist in the Scriptures !

Jesus, the "Word" who became flesh, is the builder of the spiritual temple, in which God dwells through His Spirit (1 Cor. 3 : 16; 6 : 19). This "temple", the church of the living God, has a "head". The

"head" and the foundation corner stone of this temple
is Jesus. (1 Peter 2:5,6)  The "head" of this "temple"
is not the "Word" as God, but the man Jesus Christ.

> As a man, He has God as His head.
> As a man, He was subjected to all the things
>     in which men of God ought to be subjected.
> As a man, He learned obedience. (Heb. 5:8)
> As a man, He became the mediator between
>     God and men.  (1 Tim. 2:5)

God the Father, exalted the man Jesus, and He
(the Father), subjects all things to Him. When all
things are subjected to Jesus, and when all things are
made perfect, then even the Son will be subject to the
Father, so that God may be all in all.  (1 Cor. 15 : 28)

At that time, the position of the "Christ", the
"mediator", will not be required anymore. The
"Word" will have perfected the "new creation" which
He began as "the man Jesus".

His role as "the man Jesus", will be finished.  At
that time, we will not be seeing God and Christ as two
different "heads", two different "authorities", but as
One, because "the throne (not thrones) of God and

<u>of the Lamb</u>" will be there, and the light of the Lord God (of the divinity YHWH) will be shed on us. (Rev. 22 : 1-5)

The same will also happen to the human "hierarchy". When the living Christian husband and wife meet the Lord in the air, the husband will no longer be the "head" of his wife. That "hierarchy" will be finished. <u>Thus, we see that the present condition of the "headship" is not eternal</u>.

## *The Scriptures Call Jesus God*

Now, as we study the Scriptures about Christ, we do not find anywhere --- <u>even one Scripture</u> which says that He, in His prehuman life, was an angel as the Jehovah's Witnesses proclaim. On the contrary, <u>the Scriptures state that He is God</u> ! There are many instances that record this fact; here are some of them:

First, the prophecy in Isaiah 9 : 6 calls Him "mighty God" and "everlasting Father":

"For a child is born; to us a Son is given; and His name is called ..... <u>'mighty God'</u>, the everlasting

Father ...". Here, Jesus is called "mighty God" just as YHWH is called "mighty God" in Deuteronomy 10: 17: "For Jehovah your God, He is the God of gods, and the Lord of lords; the great, the mighty, the fearful God ...".   (Also compare Nehemiah 9 : 32; Isaiah 30 : 29; 40 : 26)

Second, His name "Emmanuel", from the prophecy in Isaiah 7 : 14, means: "God with us" ! Not "a god" as Jehovah's Witnesses are saying,  but as it was written  by  Matthew in the  original  Greek text with the article "o" (the) in front of the word God, "ΜΕΘ' ΗΜΩΝ Ο ΘΕΟΣ" --- The God with us"! (Matt. 1 : 23)

Third, in Romans 9 : 5, we read from the Greek text that Jesus is:

| "Ο | ΩΝ | ΕΠΙ | ΠΑΝΤΩΝ | ΘΕΟΣ |
|------|-------------|--------------|----------|------|
| The | (always) is | above (upon) | all | God |

| ΕΥΛΟΓΗΤΟΣ | ΕΙΣ | ΤΟΥΣ | ΑΙΩΝΑΣ" |
|-----------|-----|------|---------|
| blessed | to | the | ages |

which means that Jesus is "the ever-existing God who is above all and blessed forever." !

Fourth, Thomas, the disciple of the Lord, said to Jesus that He was his "Lord and God". (John 20 : 28) Thomas  knew  very  well  the  commandment  that stated: "You  shall  not  have  any  other  gods beside Me." (Exodus 20 : 3)   Yet, he called Jesus his God !

Not "a god" as Jehovah's Witnesses claim, but as John wrote in the original Greek text with the article "o" (the) in front of the word "God":

| "Ο | ΚΥΡΙΟΣ | ΜΟΥ | ΚΑΙ | Ο | ΘΕΟΣ | ΜΟΥ" |
|-----|--------|-----|-----|-----|------|------|
| The | Lord | of mine | and | the | God | of mine |

Thomas did not say to Jesus that He was "a god", or some angel in the flesh, but "the God of mine ! ! Jesus did not correct Thomas when he called Him "the God of me", because Thomas made a true statement. Neither did John, who wrote about this incident, try to correct the words of Thomas, because John recognized and believed that Jesus was the true God. Let us read John's personal testimony: "And we know that the Son of God has come, and has given to us understanding that we might know the true One, and we are in the true One, in His Son Jesus Christ. He is the true God, and the life everlasting". (1 John 5 : 20; 1: 1-4; John 14 : 6) If you are in an angel, you cannot be in the true God !

Fifth, the apostle Peter also recognized Jesus as his God: "Simeon Peter, a slave and apostle of Jesus Christ, to those equally precious with us, having obtained faith in the righteousness of OUR GOD AND SAVIOUR, JESUS CHRIST". (2 Peter 1 : 1)

Some people, who belong to certain sects which do not believe that Jesus is God, say that the above verse is referring to two persons:

a) God, and

b) the Savior Jesus Christ.

They say that the word "and" separates the expression "of our God" from the expression "Savior Jesus Christ" ! But, the strange thing is that the same people admit that the words of 2 Peter 3 : 18, which state:

"But grow in grace and knowledge <u>of our Lord and Savior Jesus Christ</u>", refers to one person --- to the Lord Jesus Christ !

If we place both sentences side by side, word for word, we see that, according to syntax, they are both the same:

a)  our God and Savior Jesus Christ  (2 Pet. 1:1)

b)  our Lord and Savior Jesus Christ   (2 Pet. 3:18)


Let everyone judge for himself.


Finally, the apostle Paul said that we are "looking for the blessed hope and appearance of the glory of our great God and Savior, Jesus Christ, who gave Himself on our behalf, that He might redeem us from all iniquity, and purify a special people for Himself, zealous of good works". (Titus 2 : 13, 14)

The above words agree with Acts 20 : 28, where it says that <u>God purchased His church with His own blood</u> ! !

The first century Christians believed that Jesus is God. One of these Christians was Ignatius, who lived from 30 to 107 (?) A.D. Ignatius was Bishop of Antioch. He was a Christian during most of the apostle John's lifetime.

Let us see how Ignatius expressed himself about Jesus in his letter to the Ephesians:

a)  He referred to Him as "Jesus Christ our God". (First paragraph)

b)  He also referred to Him as "<u>our God, Jesus Christ</u>".  (Chapter 18)

c)  He said that "<u>God appeared in human form</u> to bring newness of eternal life".  (Chapter 19)

d)  He referred to Him as "<u>Our Lord and God, Jesus Christ</u>, the Son of the living God". (Ch. 15 from the Greek text)

In his letter to the Romans, Ignatius wrote:
". . . abundant greetings of unalloyed joy <u>in Jesus Christ our God</u> . . ." !

In his letter to the Smyrnaeans he wrote:
"<u>I praise Jesus Christ, the God who has filled you with such wisdom</u> . . ." !

The apostle Paul, in his letter to the Colossians, chapter 2 and verse 9, says, that in Jesus "dwells all the fullness of the Godhead bodily" !  ALL means ALL; <u>fullness</u> means <u>in full.</u> Whatever composes the Godhead YHWH of the Old Testament, "<u>all</u>", <u>in full, nothing less, dwells in Jesus bodily</u> !

Also, check  2 Corinthians 5 : 19 where it says that: "God was in Christ"; "in" means IN -- not "by means of" as the NWT states !

The Father, the Son and the Holy Spirit make up the one true Godhead, which, according to the Old Testament, has the name YHWH. The Father, the Son, and the Holy Spirit have one essence. Each one of these three is fully God. These three have one name; this is why the Christians are baptized "in the name (NOT NAMES) of the Father

and of the Son and of the Holy Spirit" !
(Matth. 28 :18)

Some of the modern sects such as Jehovah's Witnesses, refuse to call Jesus, YHWH. They ignore the testimony that the Holy Scriptures give on this subject. They say that the name YHWH belongs only to the Father.

The first Christians had no problem calling Jesus by the name YHWH. Let us examine the testimony of Irenaeus. Irenaeus lived from 130-200 A.D. He was a disciple of Polycarp; Polycarp was a disciple of the apostle John and lived from 65 - 155/6 A.D. Irenaeus became the Bishop of Lyones. His writings were against heresies and contained lists of all those who were bishops, in direct line from those appointed by the apostles.

He said: "The name of God or Lord is given only to Him who is called God and Lord of all; who said to Moses: 'My name is I AM. And you shall say to the Israelites, HE WHO IS has sent me to you. <u>The name of God or Lord is given also to His Son, Jesus Christ our Lord,</u> . . . And the Son says to Moses: I have come down to rescue this people.' For it is the Son who descended and ascended for the salvation of men.

Thus, through the Son who is in the Father, and has the Father in Himself, HE WHO IS has been revealed." !  (Against Heresies, III, vi : 2)

# *The Name Jesus*

The person of the Godhead YHWH, who is known as the "Word" became flesh and as a man He sacrificed Himself for our salvation. (John 1:1, 14; Matt. 1:21) That is why He was called JESUS, which means: YHWH the Savior, or YHWH is salvation.

The name "Jesus" is taken from the Greek "ΙΗΣΟΥΣ" (Jesous), which comes from the Hebrew name "Yehowshua" (Yeh-ho-shoo-ah) which is composed of two words:

a)  from the name YHWH   (Yeh - ho - vaw),  and

b)  the word "Yasha" (Yaw - shah), which means "salvation",  "save (-iour)".

## *The Godhead -- More Than One Person*

The fact that there is more than one person within the Godhead YHWH, is proven from Genesis 1 : 26 where God says: "Let us make man in Our image, according to Our likeness", in the plural form. This plural form is not used here out of "respect" or to indicate "Royalty" or "Majesty" as some say, because in Genesis 3:22, God YHWH says: "Behold ! The man has become as ONE OF US . . ." !

All the persons of the Godhead relate to the name YHWH. Since the Father is YHWH, then the only begotten Son who came out of the Father is YHWH, and so is the Holy Spirit which proceeds out of the Father ! (John 15:26; 13:3) Remember, God is light ! Whatever comes out of light is light ! Thus, whatever comes out of God is God !

This concept was clearly understood by the first Christians (yet, some modern sects are trying to tell us that the idea of one God, the Father, and of one God, the Son, and of one God, the Holy Spirit, was the result of the great "apostacy" which took place in 325 A.D. in Nicaia.)

Let us read a few words from the writings of Athenagoras, who wrote in 177 A.D. (148 years prior to 325 A.D.) defending the Christian faith at a time when the Christian Church was undergoing a great persecution. He wrote:

"I have sufficiently shown that we are not atheists since we acknowledge one God, who is uncreated, eternal, invisible, impassible, incomprehensible, illimitable. He is grasped only by mind and intelligence, and surrounded by light, beauty, spirit, and indescribable power. By Him the universe was created through His Word, was set in order, and is held together. . . But the Son of God is the Logos (the Word) of the Father, in idea and in operation; for after the pattern of Him and by Him were all things made, the Father and the Son being one. And, the Son being in the Father and the Father in the Son, in oneness and power of the Spirit . . . Since through the unity and power of the Spirit the Son is in the Father and the Father is in the Son, the Son of God is the thought (mind) and the Word (Logos) of the Father. If, however, in your superior intelligence, you should wonder what is meant by the expression 'Son', I will give you a brief explanation.

He is the First - Begotten to the Father, but not as if He were created. From the beginning, God who is Eternal mind had the Word in Himself, because He is never without the Word. Rather, the Son came forth to be formative thought and creative power for all things material . . . How can a man know his way about if he hears people decried as atheists who confess one God, the Father, and one God, the Son, and one Holy Spirit and who prove that these have power in their oneness and yet are different in their order."   (A Plea Regarding Christians, ch. 10)

## *Jesus Claims "Titles" and "Positions" which Belong Exclusively to YHWH*

Since it was YHWH the Son (while in the flesh), who  died on the cross for our salvation, He was called YHWH the Savior, Yeh-ho-shoo-ah or JOSHUA in Hebrew, ΙΗΣΟΥΣ (Jesous) in Greek and JESUS in English. Thus, the name of Jesus became our salvation because "there is salvation in no other One, for neither is there any other name under Heaven having been given among men by which we must be saved." (Acts 4 : 12)

In light of the above, we now understand the reason that the Old Testament says: "For it shall be, all who shall call on the name of YHWH shall be saved" (Joel 2 : 32), while the New Testament says that who shall call on the name of Jesus shall be saved !  (Acts 4:12;  Romans 10:13)

And while  YHWH, in the Old Testament, says: " ... to Me every knee shall bow ..." (Isaiah 45:22, 23), in the New Testament, we see that <u>every knee shall bow in the name of Jesus</u> !  (Phil. 2 : 10,11)

In Revelation 1 : 7, we read:
"Behold, He comes with the clouds, and every eye will see Him, and the ones who pierced Him, and all the tribes of the earth will wail on account of Him."

Who is the One who will come with the clouds? Who is the One on whose account all the tribes of the earth will wail? <u>Who is the One whom they pierced on the cross?</u>

When we read Matthew 24 : 30, we clearly see that this One is Jesus, the Son of man:

"And  then the sign of the Son of man will appear

in the heavens. And then, all the tribes of the land will wail. And they will see the Son of man coming on the clouds of heaven with power and much glory".

But when we read from the prophecy of Zechariah, chapter 12, starting with verse one, we see that <u>the speaker, YHWH, says</u>:

". . . And they shall look on Me whom they have pierced;" (Verse 10)

Who then is He whom they pierced on the cross? YHWH the Savior (= Jesus) !   Even from this we see the full and undivided unity of the One God ! The Father is in the Son and the Son is in the Father. (John 14 : 10)

In the New Testament, they put the value of Jesus at thirty pieces of silver; in the Old Testament they put the value of God at thirty pieces of silver. (Compare Zech. 11:12,13 with Matt. 27 : 3-10)

In Deuteronomy 10 : 17 we read:
<u>"For YHWH your God, He is . . . the Lord of lords</u>." and yet, in Revelation 17: 14 and 19 : 11-16,  we see that the "Lord of lords" is Jesus !

Is it possible that we have two Lords of lords?
--- NO, because only One is the "Lord of lords". Only
one can claim this position, so we can say that He is
"THE LORD of lords" in the singular form !

In Isaiah 44 : 6, YHWH says that He is "the First
and the Last." In Revelation 1 : 17 and 18, Jesus says:
". . . I am the First and the Last, and the living One;
and I became dead; . . . " ! Is it possible that there are
two firsts and two lasts? - NO, because ONLY ONE
can be "the" First  and ONLY ONE can be "the" Last .

In Isaiah 43 : 11, YHWH says: "I, I am YHWH;
and there is no Savior besides Me". In chapter 45 : 21
the same YHWH says:

" . . . there is no God other than Me; a just
God and a Savior; there is none except Me."

But when we read from Titus 2 : 13, 14, we hear
the apostle saying that we are "looking for the blessed
hope and appearance of the glory of our great God and
Savior Jesus Christ, who gave Himself on our behalf,
that He might redeem us" !

Surely, we do not have two Gods and two Saviors ! According to the above words of Isaiah, there is no room for two ! The Godhead is One; God is One; the Savior is One !

How is it possible that Jesus of the New Testament claims, as His own, <u>ALL</u> the above "TITLES" and "POSITIONS", which YHWH of the Old Testament exclusively claims for Himself? Because all these things belong to the Godhead YHWH ! The Father, the Son, and the Holy Spirit make up the Godhead, and as we saw previously, all the fullness of the Godhead dwells in Jesus bodily ! (Col. 2 : 9)

Later, we will examine in greater detail more "titles" and "positions" -- some major, some minor -- which belong exclusively to YHWH of the Old Testament and which Jesus claims as His own.

Everything belongs to the Father, and everything belongs to the Son ! "<u>All things</u> which the Father has are mine," said Jesus -- nothing less than the Father ! Why is this so? Because Jesus is one of the Godhead YHWH. As Jesus said, "I and the Father are one" ! (John 10:30)

## The Pre-Human Jesus is YHWH

Humans and angels, are able to talk about God, but cannot reveal Him --- cannot show Him to others! The Son, who is God, showed Him - <u>revealed Him</u> ! (John 1 : 18)

In John 14 : 7-10, Jesus said, "If you had known Me, you would have known My Father also; and from now on you do know Him, <u>and have seen Him.</u> And Philip said to Him, Lord, show us the Father, and it is enough for us. Jesus said to him, **Am I so long a time with you, and you have not known Me, Philip? The one seeing Me has seen the Father ! And how do you say, Show us the Father? Do you not believe that I am in the Father and the Father is in Me?"!**

In John 12 : 45, Jesus cried out: ". . . <u>the one seeing Me sees the One who sent Me.</u>" Only He who is equal to the Father and of the Godhead YHWH can make a statement such as this. Jesus, revealed God the Father because He is the image of the invisible God !   (Col. 1 : 15)

Whoever saw Jesus, saw the Father ! (John 14 : 7 - 10; 12 : 45). Whoever saw Jesus, saw the invisible God manifested in the flesh ! (Heb. 2 : 9; 1 Tim. 3 : 16)

In Genesis 18 : 1 - 8 we read:

"<u>And YHWH appeared to him (Abraham) by the oaks of Mamre.</u>" And Abraham bowed to the ground; they talked together; he extended his hospitality towards Him and prepared a meal for Him. (Compare with John 8 : 56 - 58)

> YHWH, whom Abraham saw by the oaks of Mamre, was JESUS, because the Bible assures us that "No one has seen God at any time." (John 1:18)

In the book of Psalms, chapter 68 and verse 18, we read the following words, which I'm sure have raised many questions:

"You have gone up on high; You have led captivity captive; You have received gifts among men; yea, to dwell among the rebellious, O Jehovah God." ! !

How is it possible to say that Jehovah went up high? Is He not the One who dwells in the highest?

The apostle Paul identifies this Jehovah who went up high; he said:

" . . .'Having gone up on high, He led captivity captive, and gave gifts to men' **but that He went up, what is it except that He also first came down into the lower parts of the earth ? He that came down is the same who also went up above all the heavens, that He might fill all things.** And He gave some to be apostles; some prophets; . . ."
(Ephesians 4 : 4 - 10)

Thus, we see that Jesus is Jehovah of Psalm 68 : 18 ! ! Therefore, the Father is YHWH and the Son is YHWH !

Men of God must have faith only in God - not in angels or anything else. But Jesus who is of the Godhead and equal to the Father (John 5 : 18) said to his disciples: " . . . believe in God, believe also in Me" (John 14 : 1). If His nature were angelic, He would not have said, "believe in Me", because He would be in complete contradiction with the laws of God in the Old Testament ! !

Jesus also said, "Believe Me that I am in the Father, and the Father is in Me." (John14:11). Yes, all the fullness of the Godhead dwells in Him bodily !

> Believing Who Jesus is (i.e. the Son of
> God and, therefore, equal to the Father),
> is a matter of life and death (John 8:24).
> Even His enemies understood that Jesus
> was making Himself equal to God by
> saying that He was the Son of God
> (because a son is always of the same
> nature as his father), and for this reason
> they wanted to kill Him ! (John 5:18;
> 10:33-39)

In Revelation, chapter 1 and verse 1, we see that Jesus Christ sent His angel to John, in order to give him the revelation.  In chapter 22 and verse 16, Jesus assures us of this again by saying: "I, Jesus, sent my angel to testify these things to you over the churches."

In verse 6 of the same chapter, we read: "... the Lord God of the holy prophets sent His angel to show His slaves what must happen quickly."  ! !

According to the above verses, who sent His angel? --- Jesus, the Lord God of the holy prophets !

What connection did Jesus Christ have with the prophets of the Old Testament? Let us read the words of apostle Peter from 1 Peter 1 : 10, 11:

"About which salvation the prophets sought out and searched out, prophesying concerning the grace for you, searching for what, or what sort of time the Spirit of Christ made clear within them; testifying beforehand of the sufferings belonging to Christ, and the glories after these." !

In Isaiah chapter 40 and verse 10, we read: "Behold, the Lord YHWH will come with strength ... Behold, His reward is with Him, and His wage before Him."

In Revelation 22 : 12, we read:
". . . behold, I am coming quickly, and My reward is with Me." The same person continues in verse 13: "I am the Alpha and the Omega, the Beginning and the Ending, the First and the Last." The identification of this speaker is revealed in verse 16, where He says: "I, Jesus" ! In verse 20, the same speaker says, "Yes, I am coming quickly . . . ", exactly the same words that He used in verse 12; and the words that follow are: "Amen, Yes, come, Lord Jesus." !

Based on the above scriptures, the question is: Who is coming and His reward is with Him? YHWH of Isaiah 40 or Jesus of Revelation 22?

Again, from the above, we see that Jesus is of the Godhead YHWH and equal to the Father, because

<u>whatever</u> the Father does, the Son does also.

In Isaiah 61 : 1 - 8, we hear someone saying: "The Spirit of the Lord YHWH is on Me, because YHWH has anointed Me . . .". The same person who speaks here continues to speak and in verse 8, he says, "<u>For I, YHWH, love judgement</u> . . .". These words were fulfilled by Jesus ! (Luke 4 : 14 - 22) Therefore, the Father is YHWH and the Son is YHWH !

## *The Pre-Human Jesus - Not a Created Angel*

If Jesus were an angel in His prehuman life (as the Jehovah's Witnesses claim), then, the New Testament wrongly asks the question: "For to which of the angels did He (the Father) ever say, 'You are my Son; today I have begotten You'?" (Hebrews 1 : 5)

If Jesus were an angel, the writer of the letter to the Hebrews would not have asked such an inappropriate question, because the answer would have been: To the "angel" Jesus ! The correct answer is: "To none of the angels", because all the angels are creatures, while Jesus is the only-begotten Son ! Jesus is the One who created the angels ! Jesus is the Eternal God, the One who existed before time began, the One who made the ages ! (Hebrews 1 : 2 from the Greek)

If Jesus, in His prehuman nature, was a created angel, then the letter to the Hebrews gives us a false testimony by telling us that "God did not subject the coming world to angels . . ." (Hebrews 2 : 5) But everything is being subjected under the feet of Jesus, because He made all things and all things were made for Him; "for all things were created in Him (Jesus), the things in the heavens, and the things on the earth; the visible and the invisible; whether thrones, or lordships, or rulers, or authorities, all things have been created through Him and for Him. And He is before all things, and all things consist in Him." ! (Col. 1 : 16, 17)

Therefore, since God *DID NOT* subject the coming world to some angel, but to Jesus (1 Cor. 15 : 27), we see that the prehuman nature of Jesus, as "the Word", had superiority above the nature of the angels !

Indeed, His nature is identical to the nature of His Father. This is why John correctly writes in his Gospel that: ". . . the Word was God." (John 1 : 1)

> The nature of every son is the same as the nature of his father !
> The substance of every son is the same as the substance of his father !

Likewise, Jesus, being the ONLY - begotten Son, is of the same nature and substance as His Father ! NO ANGEL can possibly boast of being anything like Jesus, because they are all CREATED --- NOT BORN! They are sons of God's creative power --- not sons of His substance as Jesus is !

## Arche, Ktisis, Prototokos, Protoktistos

The Greek language is very precise. Every word has its exact meaning. Those who do not know the Greek language well can be misled or can make mistakes. Because they did not pay close attention to the exactness of their own language, the Greek Jehovah's Witnesses (as I once was) allowed Jehovah's Witnesses from a foreign country to lead them astray about the nature of our Lord Jesus Christ.

They should have looked closely at the following four words:

   a)   APXH (arche = beginning, Author, power)

   b)   KTIΣIΣ  (ktisis = creation)

   c)   ΠΡΩΤΟΤΟΚΟΣ  (Prototokos = firstborn)

   d)   ΠΡΩΤΟΚΤΙΣΤΟΣ (Protoktistos = first created)

Let us examine their meaning from the Greek lexicon:

a) APXH (arche = beginning); this word does not mean only the place or time of starting, it also means: Cause, First Cause, Government and Authority. It is also the root of the word APXHΓΟΣ (Archegos = Leader). For more details about the word "APXH", see Appendix C, page 183.


In Ephesians 6 : 12, we meet the word "APXH" in its plural form: "APXAΣ" (pron. Arch-us). There, it says: "because we are not wrestling against flesh and blood, but against the rulers (APXAΣ), against the authorities . . ." !

In Luke 20 : 20, we again find the word "APXH", which has been translated into English as "power" or "control." There, it reads: " . . . so as to deliver Him (Jesus) to the power (APXH) and the authority of the governor."

Other verses which use the word "ΑΡΧΗ" with
the meaning of Authority, Government, Power, or
Leadership are: Luke 12 : 11; Romans 8 : 38; 1 Cor.
15 : 24;  Eph. 1 : 21;  3 : 10;  6 : 12;  Col. 1 : 16;
2 : 10, 15;  Tit. 3 : 1.

Jesus, the One who created all things, is the
"ΑΡΧΗ" (the Author or Head), the First Cause of the
creation, the Leader of the creation, the Authority or
Power which created all things !

Therefore, the fact that Revelation 3 : 14 calls
Jesus "... the beginning (ΑΡΧΗ) of the creation ...",
does not mean that He is the first creature created by
God; instead, it means that He is the Authority, the
First Cause, the Chief, the Author or the Head which
created all things.

b) ΚΤΙΣΙΣ   (pron. Ktisis)  =  Building, Creation.
   ΚΤΙΣΜΑ     (pron. Ktisma)= Creature, Structure,
     Creation.
   ΚΤΙΣΤΗΣ (pron. Ktistis) =Builder, Creator, God.
   ΚΤΙΣΤΟΣ  (pron. Ktistos) = A created person.
   ΠΡΩΤΟΚΤΙΣΤΟΣ (protoktistos) = First created.

The Bible DOES NOT  mention anywhere that
the "Word" is a creature.  On  the  contrary,  it states

that He is the Creator who built or created all things. Nothing was created without Him. All things were made by the "Word" who is God. (John 1 : 1 - 3)

The writer of the letter to the Hebrews, comparing the glory of Moses to the glory of Jesus, said: "For which reason, holy brothers called to be partakers of a heavenly calling, consider the Apostle and High Priest of our confession, Christ Jesus, being faithful to Him who appointed Him (to be the Apostle and the High Priest --- Hebrews 7 : 17 - 21), as also Moses in all his house. For He (Jesus) was counted worthy of more glory than Moses, by so much as the one having built the house has more honor than the house. For every house is built by someone; but He who built all things is God." (Hebrews 3 : 1 - 4)

> From the above words, we learn that the glory of Jesus is much greater than the glory of Moses, because while Moses is a creature, (the "house" of the above illustration), Jesus is the creator God who built all things !

c) ΠΡΩΤΟΤΟΚΟΣ (pron. PROTOTOKOS) = The one who is born first; First begotten; First-born.

When someone is "begotten" of his father, he is not "created" by his father! To be begotten (born) and to be created are not the same. For example, let us compare Isaak, the son of Abraham, to the altar which Abraham built. Isaak came out of Abraham --- the altar was "created" by Abraham. Isaak was Abraham's born son, being of the same form and substance as his father; the altar was Abraham's "creation". Likewise, God's Son came out of God; He was God's only begotten Son; all other beings are God's creation. God's only born Son is of the same substance, form, and nature as God --- created beings are not !

The Jehovah's Witnesses have failed to understand the above truth and they are using Col. 1 : 15 in a misleading way, in an attempt to prove that Jesus is the first creature who was created by God the Father. But, pay attention to the fact that they are using only verse 15. There, it says that Jesus is the One: "who is the image of the invisible God, the Firstborn of all creation."

"You see?" say the Witnesses. "Here it says that Jesus is the firstborn of all creation ! Therefore, He is a creature ---- part of the creation." !

In Greek, the actual word for "first created" is

"ΠΡΩΤΟΚΤΙΣΤΟΣ" (pron. PROTOKTISTOS) --- not "ΠΡΩΤΟΤΟΚΟΣ" (pron. PROTOTOKOS = first born). These two Greek words are not synonymous. The Witnesses ignore the fact that when someone is a "firstborn", he cannot be "first created", and therefore be a part of the creation. **The one Greek word refutes the other !** Yet, they insist that Jesus is called "Firstborn of all creation", <u>because</u> He is the "first creature" which God created !

But if we could ask the apostle Paul, the writer of the letter to the Colossians, "Why did you call Jesus *'firstborn'* in verse 15?" Paul would have answered, "Why do you ask me? In verse 16, beginning with the word 'because', I gave you my reason for calling Him 'firstborn'. Read my words again carefully from verses 15 to 20, paying special attention to the sentence starting with the word 'because' ":

"Who is the image of the invisible God, the Firstborn of all creation <u>because all things were created in Him</u>, the things in the heavens, and the things on the earth; the visible and the invisible; whether thrones, or lordships, or rulers, or authorities, all things have been created through Him and for Him. And He is before all things, and all things consist in Him. And He is the Head of the body, the church; who is the beginning, the Firstborn from the dead, that He be pre-eminent in all things; because all the fullness was pleased to dwell in Him, and through Him making peace by the blood of His cross, to reconcile all things to Himself through Him, whether the things on the earth, or the things in the Heavens."

From the Bible, we see that the position of a "Firstborn" was an exalted position. **It was a position of special honor and rights.** In the book of Psalms, we hear God saying about David: "And I will make him My firstborn; higher than the kings of the earth."   (Psalms 89:27) Consider that David was the last son of Jesse --- not the first ! (1 Samuel 16 : 11-13)

---

So, then, we hear the apostle Paul saying that Jesus is the "Firstborn of all creation", because all things were created in Him and for Him --- not because He is the first "creature" as Jehovah's Witnesses claim.

---

Christians accept the "because" of the apostle Paul -- not the "because" of the Watchtower Society !

Because Jesus created all creation, He holds the first place --- the first position ! He is "pre-eminent in all things" ! He is "before all things"; (It does not say "He was created before all things", but "He is before all things"). In all things, He holds the first place --- the first position, the position of a "first-born" or of the "first".

"First", according to the dictionary, is he who "precedes all others in place, time, rank, quality, etc." For this reason, we hear Jesus saying of Himself:

"... I am the First and the Last, and the Living One; and I became dead;" (Rev. 1 : 17 - 18)

So then, since we now know why the apostle Paul called Jesus "firstborn", and since we know that "firstborn" does not mean "first-created", we can no longer be misled by Jehovah's Witnesses who are degrading "the Word", the Creator God, and who insist on presenting Him as a "creature", as "another god". Christians, on the other hand, believe in one God, in one Godhead --- We are not polytheists !

Now, let us continue our study, examining:

a)   a number of "titles" and "positions" which
     belong <u>exclusively</u> to YHWH of the Old Test-
     ament, and which Our Lord, Jesus Christ, claims
     for His own;

b)   the statements made by other New Testament writ-
     ers;

c)   some of the writings of the first and second cen-
     tury Christians to learn what the disciples of the
     disciples of Jesus believed about Him;

d)   We will also use the grammar of the Greek lang-
     uage to disprove the theory of Jehovah's Wit-
     nesses about the person of Jesus Christ;

e)   We will examine a number of attributes which
     are proof of Diety and which <u>no creature</u> could
     possibly possess, but only the God by nature.

In looking at these scriptures, we will see how they
apply to the Godhead --- the Father, the Son, and the
Holy Spirit.

CHAPTER TWO

# THE CREATOR

GENESIS 1 : 1      "In the beginning God created the heavens and the earth;"

ISAIAH 44 : 24      "I am YHWH who makes all things, stretching out the heavens; I alone,"

ISAIAH 40 : 28      ". . . YHWH, the everlasting God, the Creator of the ends of the earth;"

GENESIS 2 : 7      "And YHWH God formed the man out of the dust from the ground."

JOB 33 : 4      "The Spirit of God made me, and the breath of the Almighty gives me life."

GENESIS 1 : 2,3

"and the earth being without form and empty, and darkness on the face of the deep, and the Spirit of God moving gently on the face of the waters, then God said, Let light be . . ."

PSALMS 33 : 6

"By the word of YHWH the heavens were made, and by the Spirit of His mouth all their host."

JOHN 1 : 1-3,14

"In the beginning was the Word and the Word was with God. He was in the beginning with God. All things came into being through Him, and without Him not even one thing came into being that has come into being. ... And the Word became flesh, and tabernacled among us ..."

HEBREWS 1 : 7-12   "but as to the Son (it says) ...
You, Lord, at the beginning found-
ed the earth, and the Heavens are
works of Your hands ..."

From the above scriptures we see that God the
Father created, the "Word" created, and the Spirit
created. Therefore, the creation is the work of the
Father, the Son and the Holy Spirit. Not each person
separate from and independent of the others, but all
three united in the one Godhead or one God. For this
reason, we can say that all things were created through
the Son and for the Son, as we can also say that all
things were created through God and for God!  Let us
compare the following verses:

"Because of Him (God), and <u>through Him and
for Him</u> are all things." (Romans 11 : 36)

"for all things were created in Him (the
Son)... all things have been created <u>through Him
and for Him</u>." (Col. 1 : 16)

> Both of the above scriptures point to the same
> target --- the Creator God who created all
> things for Himself.

From the above study,  we see that the Father,

the Son and the Holy Spirit is the Creator.

There is <u>ONLY ONE</u> true God --- the Creator ! It is He who said, ". . . I am YHWH who makes all things; stretching out the heavens; <u>I ALONE</u>". (Isaiah 44 : 24) If the "Word" were "another god" through whom and for whom all things were created, YHWH would not have used the expression "I ALONE"; it would not have been very considerate of God not to recognize His hard-working "Companion" who created all things for Himself !

Yes, the Father, the Son, and the Holy Spirit is the Creator God. In Psalm 33:6 we read: <u>"By the word of YHWH</u> the heavens were made, <u>and by the spirit of His mouth</u> all their hosts."

From the above scripture, we see the three persons of the Creator God: YHWH -- the Father, YHWH -- the Son (the Word), and YHWH -- the Holy Spirit.

# CHAPTER THREE

# ETERNAL

In Deutoronomy 33:27, we read that God is eternal:

"The eternal God is thy refuge . . ."

The Psalmist wrote about God:

"O Lord, You have been our dwelling-place in all generations . . . even from everlasting to everlasting You are God." (Ps. 90 : 1, 2)

Eternal, according to the dictionary, means: everlasting, existing through all time, unchangeable.

In the epistle to the Hebrews, we learn that the Holy Spirit is also eternal. (ch. 9 : 14)

The person who is eternal, has no beginning or end. What about the Son of God? Is He eternal?

In the letter to the Hebrews, chapter 7 : 1 - 3, the writer likens Melchizedek to the Son of God, and says that he was:

"without father, without mother, without genealogy, *nor beginning of days, nor having end of life, but having been like the Son of God, he remains a priest in perpetuity* (evermore)."

One of the prophecies which were given for the coming of the Messiah, says:

"And you, Bethlehem Ephratah, . . . out of you He shall come forth to Me . . . <u>and His goings forth have been from of old, from the days of eternity</u>." (Micah 5 : 2)

The above words indicate that "His goings forth have been from the days of eternity" --- <u>they do NOT say</u> that someone else or something else was in existence before Him; <u>they do NOT say</u> that there was some "other" beginning before He came into existence; <u>they do NOT say</u> that He would hold the second place in time in the universe; <u>nor do they show</u> that someone else could be older than Him! This can also be seen from John 1 : 1, where it refers to Jesus as the "Word". There, it says:

"In the beginning <u>was</u> the Word, and the Word was with God . . ." !

This verse DOES NOT SAY that in the beginning God was and later He created the Word. It states clearly that in the beginning was the Word and the Word was with God.

To put it another way, let's suppose that the following line represents time:

**BEGINNING**                                              **END**

If we try to place a dot on this Time Line to show the beginning of the "Word", we would be unable to do so because the above verse places the "Word" *before the beginning of time*; it says that in the beginning the Word "<u>was</u>" (past tense) !

**WAS**                              **BEGINNING**        **END**

The writer of the letter to the Hebrews agrees with this reasoning because he states that Jesus indeed "<u>made the ages</u>". (Ch. 1 : 2 - from the Greek) Thus, <u>in order for Jesus to have created the ages (the time), He must have been in existence before them</u> ! This proves that Jesus is eternal ! !

Since He was already in existence before the days began, no one can claim that He had a beginning of days; such a statement would be illogical.

Certain religious groups, such as the Witnesses of Jehovah, are ignoring the above scriptures. They say that in the beginning there was only God the Father, who alone is eternal and who at a later time created the Son.

In other words, they are saying that the Father is the "first" and that the Son is the "second". This statement clearly contradicts the words that our Lord said about Himself:

"I am the First and the Last, and the Living One; and I became dead; and behold, I am living forever and ever. Amen."   (Rev. 1 : 17, 18)

Likewise, the Father said, in Isaiah 44 : 6, that He is the "First and the Last." ! If the Father and the Son were two different Gods, as Jehovah's Witnesses claim, a bigger God and a lesser god, it would have been impossible for both of them to claim that they are the "first", especially if the one created the other. The second and lesser one could not also be the "first" !

If Jesus had said, "I am 'one of the First' and 'one of the Last'", it would have been a  different matter.  But instead He states that He is "the First" and "the Last", with the article "the" in front of the words "First" and "Last", which leaves no room for anyone else to be "the First" and "the Last" !

> Consequently, we conclude that all the fullness of the true Godhead YHWH, is "the First" and "the Last". The Father, His Word and His Spirit is from the beginning !

John, the disciple of the Lord, wrote about Jesus:

"THAT which was from the beginning, that which we have heard, that which we have seen with our eyes, that which we gazed upon and our hands handled, about the Word of life; (and the life was manifested, and we have seen, and bear witness, and we announce to you the eternal life, which was with the Father, and was manifested to us;)" (1 John 1 : 1, 2)

From the above words, we see that: "THAT which was from the beginning", the "Word of life", the "eternal life", which was with the Father, was revealed to men !

Jesus said, "I am . . . the life ." (John 14 : 6)

Since Jesus is "the eternal life" which was with the Father, this proves that Jesus is eternal, like the Father; otherwise, we could say that from the beginning of God's existence until the day He created the prehuman Jesus (the eternal life), God did not have eternal life! How foolish!

The same is also true with the "Word of God". If we say that the Father was in existence before the "Word", this would show us that from the beginning of His existence, until the day God created the prehuman Jesus (the Word), God was speechless --- without word ! !

A similar situation arises with the "wisdom" of God, as it is described in Proverbs, chapter 8. There, we can hear the "wisdom" of God speaking:

"YHWH possessed Me in the beginning of His way, from then, before His works. I was set up from everlasting; from the beginning, before the earth ever was . . . then I was at His side . . ." (verses 22, 23, 30)

Some identify the "wisdom" of this chapter with the Lord Jesus. (1 Cor. 1 : 24, 30) If we suppose that the "wisdom" was created by the Father and, thus, only the Father is eternal, then we could easily say that from the beginning of His existence, until the day God created the prehuman Jesus (the wisdom), God had no wisdom ! How foolish !

Some Bible translators used the word "created" in verse 22, instead of the word "possessed", and they present it as:
"YHWH created Me in the beginning of His way."

Some, like the so-called Jehovah's Witnesses, base their doctrine upon this word and say: "You see? The 'wisdom' here says that YHWH *created Me*. Therefore, God created Jesus ! Therefore, the Father must be older than Jesus" !
We observe that they base their teaching on the first half of the sentence only. The whole sentence reads:
"YHWH possessed Me in the beginning of His way, from then, BEFORE His works."

The "works" of God include everything that God brought into existence -- everything which did not exist before the day God created it. Even the first of God's works could not have said, "God created Me ... (that is) BEFORE His works"; otherwise, the sentence should read: "YHWH created Me in the beginning of His way, from then, FROM THE BEGINNING of His works" --- **NOT BEFORE !**

> The expression "before His works", within the same sentence, contradicts the idea that this "person" was one of the "works" of God. To me, this expression indicates that this "person" or "thing" was something which God "possessed" before His works.

This conclusion is correct, because God must have "possessed" or must have "had" wisdom in order for Him to know what wisdom is in order to create it ! !

Let us examine the word from the original text. The word in the original text is "qanah", (pron. kaw - naw) and it means: <u>to erect, i.e. create; to procure, to own, attain, buy, get, possess, etc.</u>

Some translators have used the expression "created Me", others "possessed Me", others "had Me" (modern Greek translation from the Hebrew), and so on.

Based upon the foregoing reasoning that **God was never without wisdom,** I conclude that the correct translations are those that use the expressions:

"*YHWH* possessed *Me* in the beginning of His way" or "*YHWH* had *Me* in the beginning of His way"

--- not "created Me" at some later time. **The "wisdom" of God is as eternal as God.**

Therefore, I conclude from the above, that as the Father is eternal, so is the Son !

# CHAPTER FOUR

# OMNIPRESENT

Another attribute of God is that <u>He is omnipresent</u>. An angel or a man can be in only one place at a time. God has no limits -- He is omnipresent ! e.g. if, let's say, ten thousand faithful talk to Him through prayer at the same time, at different places on the planet, God will hear them all. God is so great that He is present everywhere whether it is in Heaven, on earth, or any other location in the universe. **A created being is not omnipresent.**

What does the Bible say about Jesus? Does He possess this quality? Is He omnipresent? The Jehovah's Witnesses claim that His nature is angelic because He is really Michael the archangel. If this were so, He would not be omnipresent. But if He is indeed God by nature, then He certainly must be omnipresent.

Jesus said about Himself: ". . . where two or three are gathered together in My name, there I am in their midst." (Matt. 18 : 20)

Jesus, who does not lie because He is the truth, assures us that **He is omnipresent** ! "Where two or three" he said, ". . . there I am . . ." ! !

Other scriptures which prove His omnipresence are:

Matthew 28 : 20  ". . . I am with you (with all of His believers) all the days until the completion of the age." --- Even Today !

John 14 : 23  ". . . if anyone loves me, he will keep My word and My Father will love him. And We will come to him and make a dwelling place with him."

Our Lord Jesus, speaking about the Holy Spirit, said the following words in:

John 14 : 17  "the Spirit of Truth, which the world cannot receive because it does not see it nor know it. But you know it, for it abides with you, and shall be in you."

(In the Greek, the Spirit is referred to as "it", because the word "spirit" has a neuter gender. In English, this word has been translated as "he" because the Holy Spirit is a person; this is also true of God who is "a Spirit" (John 4 : 24); we refer to Him as "He" -- not "it". The fact that God is "a Spirit" does not denote that He is not a person.)

Also, the apostle Paul wrote:

> "Do you not know that you are a temple of God, and *the Spirit of God dwells in you?*" (1 Cor. 3 : 16)

King David asked God:

> "Where shall I go from Your Spirit? Or where shall I flee from Your face? *If I go up to Heaven, You are there; if I make my bed in Sheol, behold, You are there !*" (Psalms 139 : 7 - 10)

From the above scriptures, we conclude that <u>all the persons of the Godhead YHWH are omnipresent</u> !
**Therefore, since Jesus is omnipresent, He is truly God by nature ! !**

# CHAPTER FIVE

# OMNISCIENT

Another quality which belongs exclusively to God, is that <u>He is omniscient</u>. According to the dictionary, the word "omniscient" means: having infinite knowledge; knowing all things.

God is the One who knows all things. He sees into the hearts and kidneys of men, which means that He can read their innermost thoughts and intentions. No creature in the whole universe possesses this capability.

Satan and his demons trick the world through men who appear before people as if they know everything. Based on the following scriptures and upon the testimonies of former members of the occult who became Christians, I believe that demons can put an idea into the mind of a person, as a doctor can inject a drug into the blood. (Mat. 16:23; 1 Sam. 28:7; Acts 16:16,17; Mark 1:24; 5:7) In other words, I believe that when a demon introduces an idea into the mind of a man, the demon repeats it immediately to the medium who in turn repeats it aloud. Therefore,

neither the demons nor the medium are omniscient.
No one can read the hearts and kidneys of man, except
YHWH.

Jeremiah, the prophet, wrote about God YHWH:

*"But, O YHWH of hosts who judges with
righteousness, who tries the reins (kidneys) and the
heart".* (Jeremiah 11 : 20)

Also, YHWH Himself says: *"I YHWH search the
heart, I try the reins (kidneys), even to give to each
man according to his ways, according to the fruit of
his doings."* (Jerem. 17 : 10)

Now then, since we saw that the omniscient YHWH
is the One who tries the kidneys and the hearts, let us
read from   Revelation 2 : 18 - 23 where it says:
*". . . These things says the Son of God . . . all the
churches will know that* <u>*I am the One searching the
kidneys and hearts*</u>*. And I will give to each of you
according to your works."* ! !

Here, we hear Jesus claiming that He is the one
who searches kidneys and hearts, and that
He will give to each one according to his works ! !
He uses exactly the same words as God YHWH in
Jeremiah 17 : 10.

Who then is Jesus? --- The omniscient God!  The disciples of the Lord and others, such as Matthew, Mark, Luke, and John, wrote that Jesus knew all things;  let us read some of their words:

"Now we know ... *You know all things*." (John 16:30)

"... *Lord, You perceive all things*;" (John 21:17)

"But Jesus Himself did not commit Himself to them, because He knew all ... *He knew what was in man*." (John 2:24)

"And Jesus, *perceiving the thought of their heart ...*" (Luke 9:47)

*"But He knew their thoughts . . ."*    (Luke 6:8)

"And immediately *when Jesus perceived in His spirit that they so reasoned within themselves ...*" (Mark 2:8)

*"And Jesus knew their thoughts, ..."* (Matthew 12:25)

*"And Jesus knowing their thoughts ..."* (Matthew 9:4).

The apostle Paul wrote:

"Therefore judge nothing before the time, until *the Lord come, who both will bring to light the hidden things of darkness, and will make manifest the counsels of the hearts;* and then shall every man have praise from God." (1 Corin. 4 : 5)

From the above testimonies of those who lived with the Lord Jesus when He was on earth, we are assured that **Jesus Christ is indeed omniscient.**

Now, let us read from 1 Cor. 2 : 10 to find out what it says about the Holy Spirit:

"But God revealed them to us by His Spirit, for <u>the Spirit searches all things, even the deep things of God</u>." !

Thus, we see that the Holy Spirit is also omniscient! (Also check Romans 8 : 26)

So then, we conclude that:

the Father is omniscient,
the Son is omniscient, and
the Holy Spirit is omniscient !

Therefore, since Jesus is omniscient, and since being omniscient belongs only to God by nature, then **Jesus is God by nature !**

# CHAPTER SIX

# OMNIPOTENT

"Omnipotent", means: almighty, all-powerful, having unlimited power or authority.

"ΠΑΝΤΟΚΡΑΤΩΡ" (pron. Pantokrator) in Greek, found in Rev.1:8, (in the Greek text) is another word for almighty. The literal meaning is: "<u>He who has the power to hold all things</u>."

"Omnipotence" means: the state or quality of being omnipotent; having <u>absolute authority</u>, to be able to do all things.

"Absolute authority", is the authority which is unbound, independent, unlimited, total, full, complete. Only the God by nature is Almighty --- "Pantokrator" in Greek. (Genesis 17 : 1;  35 : 11)   Only He has the power to "hold all things".  No creature has the power that can be compared with the omnipotence of God.

Satan can imitate the powers of God, but only up

to a point and according to the permissive will of God, (as we know from the cases of Job and of Moses who fought the sorcerers of Pharaoh), because he is not God by nature. Therefore, he is not almighty. (Exodus 7 : 10 - 22)

Is our Lord, Jesus Christ, almighty? The Jehovah's Witnesses, are trying, with persistence and zeal, to prove that the Son is another god, less powerful than God the Father. They say that only the Father is almighty, while the Son is just a "mighty god".

In their attempt to prove this, they refer to Isaiah 9 : 6, where it says about Jesus:

"For a child is born; to us a son is given; and the government is on His shoulder; and His name is called . . . mighty God . . ."

"You see?" say the Witnesses, "The prophecy here says that Jesus is a 'mighty god' -- not almighty. Only the Father is almighty." !

In their darkness, because they have not seen the glory of the light which came into the world to die for them, they have failed to notice that the Bible also uses exactly the same expression for God the Father. The word which has been used in the above prophecy (in the original text) for the word "mighty" is "gibbowr" or "gibbor". The same word is found in Nehemiah 9 : 32, where it says:

"And now our God ... the mighty (gibbowr) ..." !

The same word also appears in Jeremiah 32 : 17 and 18, where it says:

"Ah, Lord YHWH!  You have made the heavens and the earth by Your great power . . . not any thing is too difficult for You . . . the mighty (gibbowr) God, YHWH of hosts is His name, . . ." ! !

Jeremiah here calls God, "<u>mighty</u>" --- <u>not almighty</u>, and he says that "not any thing is too difficult" for Him!  (Also read Deuter. 10 : 17)

Let Jehovah's Witnesses ask themselves:

Is there any thing that is too difficult for Jesus, just because the prophecy of Isaiah calls Him "mighty God" and not almighty? Does the fact that Nehemiah, Jeremiah, and others who call God YHWH "mighty", belittle Him?

The answer to both questions is, "No !" Therefore, this doctrine of theirs is unreasonable and inconsistent.

The Son is as mighty as the Father; as almighty as the Father ! The Son Himself said:

". . . whatever that One (the Father) does, these things also the Son likewise does."! **Nothing less !** (John 5 : 19 --- from the Greek).

As we discussed earlier, "omnipotence" means having unlimited power, full or absolute authority. The resurrected man Jesus, said:

"All authority in Heaven and on earth was given to Me." (Matt. 28 : 18)

"All" means "ALL" -- unlimited; it does **NOT** mean "some" !

Jehovah's Witnesses will argue that Jesus did not always have "all authority", because in the above words He said that this "was given" to Him. They forget that the "Word" humbled Himself, veiling His Godly glory and power, in becoming flesh (John 1 : 1 - 4, 14; Philippians 2 : 6 -11). In Matth. 28 : 18, God did not give "all authority" to the "Word", but to the humbled and resurrected man Jesus.

Jesus was not glorified with more glory than that which He had in His prehuman existence as God. It was not the "Word", but the man Jesus who said to His Father:

**"And now Father, glorify Me with Yourself, with the glory which I had with You before the existence of the world."** !  (John 17 : 5)

In the prophecy of Isaiah 9 : 6, it says: ". . . and the dominion is upon His shoulder," !

"Dominion" means: sovereign authority.

The above prophecy does not say that "some dominion" or authority is upon His shoulder, but **"the dominion"**. He bears upon Himself the absolute authority.

The size of His authority or His omnipotence was also made manifest in the case of His resurrection. He said: ". . . Destroy this temple, and in three days I will raise it up." (John 2 : 19 - 22)

> From His words, we are made aware that He has the omnipotence, the absolute authority, to raise Himself from the dead !

The omnipotence in the case of the resurrection, belongs to all the fullness of the Godhead, because not only did Jesus resurrect Himself, but the Father also resurrected Him (Acts 2 : 24; 4 : 10) through the power of the Holy Spirit !

As we read Luke 1:35; Acts 1:8, and Rom. 15:13, 19, we observe that omnipotence belongs also to the Holy Spirit.

The Son is as omnipotent or almighty as is the Father. He said to His Father:

"And <u>ALL</u> my possessions are thine and thy possessions mine and I have been glorified in them." (John 17 : 10 --- *emphasized from the Greek.*)

He also said:

"<u>ALL things whatsoever the Father hath are My own</u>." (John 16:15 --- emphasized from the Greek.)

"<u>ALL</u>" said Jesus; **nothing less than the Father.** "ALL" includes "<u>the might</u>", which belongs "To Him sitting on the throne, and to the Lamb . . . for ever and ever." (Revelation 5 : 13)

Speaking of Jesus, the following words indicate that He is as almighty as the Father:

"Who (Jesus) being the shining splendor of His (God's) glory and the express image of His (God's) essence, and <u>bearing (holding) up all things by the</u> <u>word of His power.</u>"    (Hebrews 1:3)


**Pause and consider:**

Since Jesus is the one who "holds up all things" with the word of His power, then, without doubt, He is Almighty --- "Pantokrator" ! !

# CHAPTER SEVEN

# The Lord of Hosts

"The Lord of hosts", is the translation of the YHWH tsaba (pronounced tsaw - baw), from the original text of the Old Testament, and it means: "YHWH of the angelic armies (hosts)."

This expression is being used exclusively for YHWH, the God of Israel, as it is found in Jeremiah 16 : 9, where it says:

"For so says Jehovah (YHWH) of hosts, the God of Israel;" (Also read Jer. 27:21).

**No creature can boast that he is the Lord (YHWH) of hosts.**

Is Jesus, the Word, "the Lord (YHWH) of hosts"? If He is part of the creation, the answer is, NO ! But if He is God by nature, and One of the true Godhead YHWH, the answer is: YES ! Let us examine this point from the Holy Scriptures.

The prophet Isaiah describes to us the wonderful experience he had when he saw the Lord of hosts:

". . . I saw", he says to us, "the Lord sitting on a

**79.**

throne, high and lifted up. And His train filled the temple. Above Him stood the seraphs . . . And one cried to the other  and said, <u>Holy, holy, holy is Jehovah (YHWH) of hosts</u>;  all the earth is full of His glory ! . . . Then I said, Woe is me !  For I am cut off; . . . for my eyes have seen the King, Jehovah (YHWH) of hosts . . . And I heard the voice of YHWH saying, Whom shall I send, and who will go for us? Then I said, I am here. Send me !  And He said, Go and tell the people, Hearing you hear, but do not understand; and seeing you see, but do not know . . . that he (this people) not see with his eyes,  and hear with his ears, and understand with his heart and turns and one heals him . . ."   (Isaiah 6 : 1 - 10)

Who is this YHWH of hosts that Isaiah saw? Whose glory did Isaiah see? Who was the One that Isaiah called, "The Lord of Hosts."?

Some will say, "God the Father". But how is it possible for this to be true, while the Scriptures assure us that "No one has seen God at anytime."?  (1 John 4: 12). The Scriptures cannot lie; therefore, whose glory did Isaiah see?

John,  the disciple of our Lord Jesus,  referring to

the above words of Isaiah, in his Gospel (chapter 12, verses 37 - 41), talks about Jesus saying:

"But though He had done so many miracles before them, they did not believe in Him . . . because Isaiah said again, 'He has blinded their eyes and has hardened their heart, that they might not see with the eyes, and understand with the heart, and be converted, and I should heal them.' <u>Isaiah said these things when He saw His glory and spoke about Him</u>." !

> Therefore, the Lord of hosts whom Isaiah saw was the "Word" (Jesus) in one of His pre-human appearances.

We conclude then that the Son is the Lord of hosts, as the Father is also the Lord of hosts ! The Son is fully God and God by nature, as the Father is also fully God and God by nature.

<u>Jesus shares ALL things with the Father</u> ! The Son, the man Jesus, is, one could say, the "partner" or "associate" of the Father. This is exactly how YHWH calls Jesus, His Shepherd, in the prophecy which He gave about Him in Zechariah, chapter 13 and verse 7 :

"O sword, awake against My Shepherd, even against
the man that is my associate, says YHWH of hosts.
Strike the Shepherd, and the sheep will be scattered"
(Also read Matt. 26 : 31;  Mark 14 : 27)

    As partners, they share:

**The Throne !**    "And he showed me a pure river of
water of life . . . coming forth out of
the throne of God and of the Lamb.
(Rev. 22:1-4)  Here,  it does not refer
to "thrones" in the plural, but to the
"throne" which belongs to God and to
the Lamb !

**The Name !**    ". . . baptizing them in the name of the
the Father and of the Son and of the
Holy Spirit;" (Matt. 28 : 19) Here, it
does not refer to names in the plural,
but  to the "name"  which belongs to
the Father and to the Son  and  to  the
Holy Spirit."

**The Kingdom !**    "... The Kingdoms of the world became our Lord's and of His Christ ..."
(Rev. 11 : 15)

The Worship !    "... they will be **priests of God and of Christ** ... "    (Rev. 20 : 6)
The duty of the priests is to worship God. Also read Daniel 7 : 13,14, where it says that <u>all the peoples, the nations, and the languages will worship (serve) the Son of man.</u>

The Blessing !    "And every creature which is in Heaven, and in the  earth,  and  underneath
The Honor !    the earth, and the things  that  are  on the sea,  and  the things in all of them,
The Glory !    I heard saying:  <u>To Him sitting on the throne, and to he Lamb</u> be **the bless-**
The Might !    **ing** and **the honor,** and **the glo-ry** and **the might** for ever and ever."   (Rev. 5 : 15)


In John 5:23, Jesus said that all men should:
". . . honor the Son, even as they honor the Father . . ."
--- not less than the Father, but exactly  the  same, because He said: ". . . <u>as they honor the Father</u> . . ." !

Why as they honor the Father?  **Because Jesus**

is equal to the Father, One of the true
Godhead, fully God, and God by nature !

CHAPTER EIGHT

# UNCHANGEABLE

Unchangeable means: immutable; the one who does not change.

In Malachi 3:6, we hear God saying about Himself: ". . . I am YHWH, I change not."

The Psalmist revealed that God is unchangeable:

"O my God, ... Your years are through the generation of generations. You have laid the foundation of the earth of old; and the heavens are the work of Your hands. They shall perish, but You shall endure; ... they shall be changed. But You are He (the same --- emphasized from original text. Psalms 102 : 24 - 27)

The writer of the letter to the Hebrews, in the first chapter and verses 7 - 12, says that the above words of Psalm 102, were written about the Lord Jesus as the Son of God ! Let us follow his words, starting with verse 7:

"And as to the angels, He said, "Who makes His angels spirits, and His ministers a flame of fire; but

**as to the Son,** "Your throne O God, is forever and ever, . . ." and, "<u>You, Lord, at the beginning founded the earth,</u> and the heavens are works of Your hands. They shall vanish away, but you will continue; and they will all become old, like a garment . . . and <u>they shall be changed. But You are the same</u> . . ." !

Finally, as we read Hebrews 13 : 8, we see once again that: "Jesus Christ (is) <u>the same yesterday and today and forever.</u>" !


**Therefore, the Son is unchangeable, as the Father is unchangeable.**

CHAPTER NINE

# LIGHT

The Psalmist said:

"YHWH is my light and my salvation." (ch. 27 : 1)

The prophet Isaiah wrote:

"... YHWH shall become thine age - abiding light ..."
(Ch. 60 : 19 -- emphasized)

John, the disciple of Christ, said:

". . . <u>God is light</u> , and no darkness is in Him ---
none." (1 John 1 : 5), and ". . . <u>the light has come
into the world</u>". (John 3 : 19)  He did not say that "a
lesser" light than the light of the Father has come into
the world; he said that "the light has come into the
world." !

Jesus said:

". . . I am the Light of the world." (John 8 :
12), and ". . . Yet a little while the Light is with you.
Walk while you have the Light, that darkness not
overtake you." (John 12 : 35)

John did not say that Jesus was a
reflection of God's light, neither did he

**say that He was an imitation; he said that Jesus Himself was "the true light" !**

Let us read his words from John 1:4, 5, 9, and 10:

"In Him was life, and the life was the light of men, and the light shines in the darkness, and the darkness did not overtake it . . . <u>He was the true Light, which enlightens every man coming into the world.</u> He was in the world, and the world came into being through Him; yet the world did not know Him.

What grandeur ! What glory ! The Father is Light and the Son is Light ! **The "true Light" came into the world, and the world was made through Him!**

None of the angels, none of the creatures, can be the true light. None can have this glory ! None, but God alone !

> The light of an angel or any other creature is not enough to enlighten every man coming into the world ! The God by nature alone is so great, so fearful and so wonderful ! (Revel. 21 : 23)

CHAPTER TEN

# LIFE

God is life. God is the source or fountain of life.

In Psalm 36 : 7 - 9, we read:

". . . O God ! . . . with You is the fountain of life; in your light, we see light."

In John 1 : 4 we read about Jesus: "In Him was life, and the life was the light of men." !

From 1 John 1 : 1 - 4, we learn that ". . . the life was revealed, and we have seen . . . and we announce to you the everlasting life which was with the Father, and was revealed to us."

None of the angels, none of the creatures could be "the everlasting Life which was with the Father" ! All the angels and the rest of the creatures needed "the everlasting Life" to bring them into being. Only the God by nature is "the Life" ! **Therefore, Jesus, "the everlasting life", is God by nature !**

The apostle John said again:

". . . we know that the Son of God has come, and has given us an understanding that we might know the true one, and we are in the true one, in His Son Jesus

Christ. This is the true God, and the life everlasting."
(1 John 5 : 20)

None of the angels or any other creature can say,

**"I am the Life." -- The Lord Jesus is !**
(John 14 : 6;  Col. 3 : 4)

Jesus does not have "life in Himself" only for
Himself, but He also is the "resurrection and the Life"
for others.  (John 5 : 26;  11 : 25)

Jesus said, "I am the Bread of life". He also said,
"I am the living Bread that came down from Heaven.
If anyone eats of this Bread,  he will live forever" !
And, "The one partaking of My flesh and drinking of
My blood has everlasting life, and I will raise him up
at the last day." (John 6:48, 51, 54)

What wonderful claims ! "I am the Bread of life ...
if  anyone eats of this bread, he will live forever".
From this we see that the Lord Jesus is the source and
the sustainer of life !

The Father gives life, the Son gives life, and the
Holy Spirit gives life.   (2 Cor. 3 : 16; Rom. 8 : 11)

In Revelation 22 : 1, we read:

"And he showed me a pure river of water of life
bright as crystal, coming forth out of **the throne of
God and of the  Lamb."**

Here we see that the river of the water of life springs out of the throne of God and of the Lamb (Jesus) ! **Therefore, the Son is as much the fountain of life as is the Father !**

The Holy Spirit is also identified with the river of life. Jesus said: ". . . if anyone thirsts, let him come to Me and drink. The one believing in Me, as the Scripture said, "Out of his belly will flow rivers of living water." But He said this concerning the Spirit, whom the ones believing in Him were about to receive;" (John 7 : 37 - 39)

From the foregoing we see that all the Godhead, (the Father, the Son, and the Holy Spirit), is the Fountain of Life ! Therefore, since the Lord Jesus Christ is the Fountain of Life, He is God by Nature !

CHAPTER ELEVEN

# The First and the Last

He who is the fountain of life, is also "the first" in the whole universe.

In Isaiah 41 : 4, we hear God saying: "I YHWH am the first and the last; I am He."

In Isaiah 48 : 12, He repeats: "... I am the first ... I am the last" !

In Isaiah 44 : 6, we read: "So says YHWH, the King of Israel, and his Redeemer, YHWH of hosts: I am the First and I am the Last; and there is no God except Me." !

According to the above, only one is "the first" and "the last" --- the Lord, YHWH of hosts. There is no room for any other god !

Only He who is the fountain of life, the Creator of all, is the "First." ! Even the first creature that God created, holds the second place ! That creature can not claim that he is "the first" ! But Jesus, who is the

92.

fountain of life, the Creator of all, One of the Godhead YHWH, and, of course, fully God and equal to the Father, claims for Himself this position which belongs only to the One who is God by nature.

In Revelation 1 : 17, 18, we hear Jesus saying: "... I am the First and the Last, and the Living One; and I became dead; and, behold, I am living forever and ever ..." !

In chapter 2 and verse 8, He repeats: "These things says the First and the Last, who became dead, and lived;"

> Indeed, Jesus claims for His own, this unique position. He said that He is "the First and the Last" - NOT "the second" and "the one before the last" as Jehovah's Witnesses portray Him with their theory.

Therefore, whatever the Father is, the Son is also ! Whichever person of the Godhead speaks, has the right to say that He is the First and the Last, and **the only true God** !

# CHAPTER TWELVE

# SAVIOUR

In the Old Testament we hear God YHWH saying: "I, I am YHWH; and there is no Savior besides Me."   (Isaiah 43 : 11)

In chapter 45 of the same book, and verse 15, we read: "Truly, You are a God who hides Himself, O God of Israel, the Savior." Also, in verse 21, God repeats that   ". . . there is no God other than Me; a just God and a Savior."

In Hosea 13 : 4, God repeats: ". . . I am the Lord thy God from the land of Egypt, and thou shalt know no god but me: for there is no saviour beside me."

However, while we hear God YHWH saying: "... there is no Savior besides Me", the apostle Paul said to the Philippian Christians, "... our citizenship is in Heaven, from where we also wait for a Savior, the Lord, Jesus Christ." ! (Chapter 3 : 20)

In his epistle, the apostle Peter wrote: "But grow in grace and knowledge of our Lord and Savior, Jesus Christ. To Him be the glory, both now and to the day of eternity ..."    (2 Peter 3 : 18)

Again while God YHWH says: "... there is no God other than Me; a just God and a Savior", the apostle Peter talks to us about "the righteousness of our God and our Savior, Jesus Christ" !
(2 Peter 1 : 1)

The apostle Paul wrote that we are "looking for the blessed hope and appearance of the glory of our great God and Savior, Jesus Christ, who gave Himself on our behalf ..." !    (Titus 2 : 13,14)


**Thus, we see again that whatever the Father is, so is the Son !**

# CHAPTER THIRTEEN

# THE LORD OF LORDS

The title, "The Lord of lords", shows that there is only One who can be "The Lord" above all the other lords. It excludes the existence of a second person who can hold this position, because, it does not say "the Lords" in the plural form, but "the Lord" in the singular form !

According to the Old Testament, only God YHWH is the Lord of lords: "For YHWH your God, He is the God of gods, and the Lord of lords." (Deut. 10:17)

In the book of Psalms, chapter 136 and verses 1 - 3, we read:

"O give thanks to YHWH, for He is good ...

O give thanks to the God of gods ...

O give thanks to the Lord of lords ...".

However, the New Testament, in the book of Revelation, tells us that **Jesus is the one who holds this position:** "... the Lamb (Jesus) will overcome them because He is the Lord of lords and

King of kings ..."   (ch. 17 : 14)

In chapter 19 : 11 - 16, it says: "And He  (Jesus) has . . . a name . . . written: KING OF KINGS AND LORD OF LORDS"

> No creature possesses the positions and titles which exclusively belong to the One God !

The  Son, who  is  not  a  creature, but God by nature, is whatever the Father is !  And yet, we  do  not  have two "Lords  of  lords", but One:   The  true  Godhead YHWH !

## CHAPTER FOURTEEN

# THE SHEPHERD

In the Old Testament, God YHWH is "the shepherd":

"YHWH is my shepherd; I shall not want." (Psalms 23 : 1)

"Behold, the Lord YHWH will come with strength, ... His reward is with Him ... He shall feed His flock like a shepherd; He shall gather lambs ... in His bosom carry them; those with young He will lead." (Isaiah 40 : 10, 11)

Jesus said: "I am the good shepherd".

He also said:
". . . and I lay down My Soul for the sheep. And I have other sheep . . . I must also lead those . . . and there will be one flock, one Shepherd,". (John 10: 7 - 16)

In John 16 : 13, we read about the Holy Spirit: ". . . the Spirit of the truth . . . **He will guide** you into all truth."

We do not have two Shepherds but One !

We do not have three leaders but One !

**Who leads us like a Shepherd? -- The true Godhead YHWH !**

## CHAPTER FIFTEEN

# THE JUDGE

In Genesis 18 : 25, 26, we read: ". . . <u>The judge of all the earth, shall He not do right? And YHWH said</u>, if I find fifty righteous within the city, in Sodom, then I will spare all the place because of them."

In Acts 10 : 40 - 42, we read about Jesus: "God raised up this One the third day, and . . . <u>it is He</u> who has been marked out by God <u>to be judge of the living and the dead</u>."

Once more we see that whatever the Father is, so is the Son !

Other Scriptures that speak about the "Judge" are: Matthew 25:31-46; Acts 17:31; Rev. 20:12,13; Rom. 2:16; 3:6; Hebrews 13:4; Revelation 18:8, 20; John 5:19 - 27. Read especially Heb. 4:12,13, where it states that everyone will have to give an account of their actions to the "Word".

CHAPTER SIXTEEN

# THE FORGIVER OF SINS

God YHWH emphatically says:

"I am He who blots out your trespasses for My sake; . . ."    (Isaiah 43 : 16 - 25)

In the Gospel of Mark, we read:

"And ... Jesus said to the paralytic, Child, your sins are forgiven to you. But some of the scribes were sitting there, and reasoning  in their hearts, ... Who is able to forgive sins, except One, God?" (Ch. 2 : 5 - 12)

Whatever authority the Father has,  the Son has also -- NOTHING LESS THAN THE FATHER.

# CHAPTER SEVENTEEN

# THE ONE WHO RECEIVES AND ANSWERS PRAYER

From ancient times, faithful men of the true God were praying to Him. Even Jesus, when He was on the earth as a man in the flesh, was praying to the heavenly Father.

In Acts 7 : 59, we read something new: "And they stoned Stephen, invoking and saying, Lord Jesus receive my spirit" ! These words clearly state that **Stephen prayed to Jesus and asked Him to receive his spirit** ! If Jesus were an "angel" (as Jehovah's Witnesses are trying to prove), Stephen would not have prayed to Him. Stephen, did not entrust his spirit into the hands of an "exalted angel", because he knew that at death, the spirit of man returns to God who gave it ! (Ecclesiastes 12 : 7)

Also, Jesus Himself said:

"And whatever you may ask in My Name, this I

will do, that the Father may be glorified in the Son. If you ask anything in My Name, I will do it." (John 14 : 13, 14)

From the above, *we see that since Jesus receives and also answers prayers, because He said, "I will do it", then He is God.*

None of the created beings has the capacity to listen to all the prayers of all the faithful at once, and to answer them all. **Jesus can, because He is God by nature !**

# CHAPTER EIGHTEEN

# THE KING OF KINGS

According to the Old Testament, YHWH is the King of Israel. He is the "eternal King", the "King of glory", and the "King of kings". Let us read the following scriptures:

"for our help is of the Lord; and of the Holy One of Israel, our king."   (Psalms 89:18 --- Septuagint)

"The LORD (YHWH) is King forever and ever . . ." (Psalms 10:16)

"Who is he, this King of glory? The LORD (YHWH) Almighty --- he is the King of glory." (Psalms 24:7-10)

From 1 Timothy 6:15,16, we see that God is the "King of kings": "which God will bring about in his own time --- God, the blessed and only Ruler, the King of kings and the Lord of lords, who alone is immortal and who lives in unapproachable light, whom no one has seen  or can see.  To him be honor and might forever. Amen." (NIV)

Nevertheless, in the New Testament we read that the "King of Israel", the "Lord of glory" and the "King of kings" is the Lord Jesus Christ:

". . . the great crowd . . . shouting, Hosanna ! Blessed is he who comes in the name of the Lord ! . . . the King of Israel !" (John 12:12,13)

"None of the rulers of this age understood it, for if they had, they would not have crucified the Lord of glory." (1 Corin. 2:8)

"On his robe and on his thigh he has this name written: KING OF KINGS AND LORD OF LORDS." (Revel. 19:6)

Also read Psalms 95:3; Matthew 25:34; 27:1, 2, 29, 37; 2:2; Luke 19:38; John 1:50; 12:15; Acts 17:7; I Tim. 1:17.

From the above study we learn, once more, that the Son holds all the titles and the positions which belong to God; therefore, Jesus is God.

## CHAPTER NINETEEN

# STUMBLING STONE

"Sanctify YHWH of hosts Himself, and let Him be your fear; and let Him be your dread. And <u>He shall be</u> for a sanctuary, and for <u>a stone of stumbling</u>, and for a rock of falling to the two houses of Israel; . . ." (Isaiah 8 : 13, 14)

CONSIDER: **How was it possible for** <u>**YHWH Himself**</u> **to become a stumbling stone to Israel? Was He not their God?**

"For they stumbled at the stone - of - stumbling, (Jesus) as it has been written, 'Behold, I place in Zion a Stone - of - stumbling, and a Rock - of - offense; and everyone believing on Him will not be put to shame.'" (Romans 9 : 31-33; also read Ch. 10 : 9 - 11)

The Father is a stone - of - stumbling, and so is the son ! **Whatever the Father is, so is the Son, for the Father is in the Son, and the Son is in the Father.** (John 14 : 7 - 10)

# CHAPTER TWENTY

# THE HEALER

In Psalms 103 : 2, 3, we see that He who has the power to heal every sickness is God YHWH !

Let's read it:

"Bless YHWH, O my soul, and forget not all His rewards; who forgives all your iniquities; who heals all your diseases;" !

However, when the apostle Peter spoke to Aeneas, he said to him:

". . . Aeneas, **Jesus the Christ heals you**; rise up and spread (make thy bed) for yourself" ! (Acts 9 : 34)

In the book of the prophet Isaiah, chapter 6 and verses 8 - 10, we hear God YHWH saying:

". . . Go and tell this people, Hearing you hear but do not understand; and seeing you see, but do not know. Make the heart of this people fat, and make his ears heavy, and shut his eyes, that he not see with his eyes, and hear with his ears, and understand with his heart, and turn and one heals him."

**107.**

The above prophecy, was fulfilled by the Lord Jesus, and it is recorded in Matthew 13 : 13 - 15. There, the words of the above prophecy are repeated in the same way exactly, except for the last sentence. That sentence now reads: ". . . <u>and I heal them</u>." !

Now, if we read Acts 28 : 25 - 27, we will see that the same prophecy is repeated with exactly the same words; in the last sentence, it says again: "... and <u>I heal them</u>", except that this time, the speaker is the Holy Spirit ! !    (verse 25)

From the above, we see that all the fulness of the Godhead, that is the Father, the Son and the Holy Spirit is the healer !

## CHAPTER TWENTY - ONE

# TO WHOM DOES THE GLORY BELONG ?

"Glory", means: honor, value, praise, splendor.

The degree of glory varies from man to man or from angel to angel; it depends on one's social position.

The glory of God is unique. **None of the created beings can possess or even share God's glory.**

God YHWH is a jealous God. (Exodus 34 : 14) He does not share the glory which belongs to Him alone. Let us examine what He says about this in Isaiah 42 : 8:

"I am YHWH; that is My name; and I will not give My glory to another . . ." !

And in Isaiah 48 : 11, He repeats: "... I will not give My glory to another." !

## 110.     To Whom Does the Glory Belong?

When we read the Old Testament, we see that God YHWH is called: "the King of glory." !

"Lift up your heads, O gates; and be lifted up, O everlasting doors; and the King of glory shall come in. Who is this King of glory? YHWH strong and mighty. YHWH mighty in battle ! Lift up your heads, O gates; even lift up, O everlasting doors; and the King of glory shall come in. Who is this King of glory? YHWH of hosts, He is the King of glory" !
(Psalm 24 : 7 - 10)

In Psalm 29 : 3, we read:

"The voice of Jehovah is on the waters; the God of glory thunders; . . ." !

But reading from the New Testament, we see that Jesus is called: "the Lord of glory", and the Holy Spirit: "the Spirit of glory" ! !

The apostle Paul wrote the following to the Corinthian Christians:

". . . we speak the wisdom of God in a mystery . . . which not one of the rulers of this age has known. For if they had known, they would not have crucified **the Lord of glory.**" !
(1 Corin. 2: 7, 8)

The apostle Peter said:
"... you are blessed, because the Spirit of God and of the glory rests on you." ! (1 Peter 4:14 - from the Greek).

The same apostle, who knew very well how jealous God YHWH is, as far as "the glory" is concerned, wrote the following: "... grow in ... knowledge of our Lord and Savior, Jesus Christ, <u>To Him be the glory,</u> both now and to the day of eternity." ! !
(2 Peter 3 : 18)

To whom then does the glory belong? To the Father or to the Son? In Revelation 5 : 13, we read: "... every creature which is in Heaven and in the earth, and underneath the earth, and the things that are on the sea, and the things in all of them, I heard saying: <u>To Him sitting on the throne, and to the Lamb be . . . the glory . . . forever and ever.</u>" ! !

Consider: If Jesus were a being created by God (as Jehovah's Witnesses claim) then, He should also say the above words to Himself, because it says, "... <u>every creature which is in Heaven</u> ... I heard saying: ... **to the Lamb be** ... **the glory** ... for ever and ever." !

# 112.　To Whom Does the Glory Belong ?

If Jesus were a "creature" of God, outside the true Godhead YHWH, then, God YHWH would not have shared with Him His glory !　(Isaiah 42 : 8; 48 : 11)

From the above, we see that the glory belongs to all the fulness of the Godhead:

To the Father, the *"King of glory"*,

To the　Son, the *"Lord of glory"*, and

To the Holy Spirit,　the *"Spirit of glory"* !

Once again, we have very compelling proof that Jesus is equal to the Father, sharing all things with Him, because He is One of the Godhead, fully God and God by nature.

CHAPTER TWENTY - TWO

# THE ONE WHO
# RECEIVES WORSHIP

Now, we have come to the most crucial topic in our study of the person of our Lord, Jesus Christ.

Should Jesus be worshipped?

If Jesus were a created being, a "creature" of God, and, of course, a part of the creation, the answer is: NO ! If Jesus were "another" god, "lesser" than the Father, and outside the Godhead YHWH, the answer is: NO ! God is against those "who . . . worshipped and served the created thing rather than the Creator, who is blessed forever." (Romans 1 : 25 - from the Greek)

If Jesus were created by God, and if He were a part of the creation, then, the worship of His person would constitute idolatry ! !

If Jesus is not God by nature, and one of the Godhead YHWH, then the worship of His person, as "another god", would constitute an act of disobedience of the first two Commandments, which God YHWH gave to Moses:

"You shall not have any other gods beside Me. You shall not make a graven image for yourself, of any likeness which is in the heavens above, or which is in the earth beneath, or which is in the waters under the earth; you shall not bow to them, and you shall not serve them; for I am YHWH your God, a jealous God . . ."   (Exodus 20 : 3 - 5)

"To bow" means: to bend the head or body in respect or recognition;  to express religious respect.

"To worship" means "to serve". ("Worship" in Greek is "ΛΑΤΡΕΥΩ" = Latrevo , from the noun "ΛΑΤΡΙΣ" = Latris, which means "a hired menial"). Check STRONG'S EXHAUSTIVE CONCORDANCE OF THE BIBLE, in the Greek Dictionary, page 44, word no. 3000.

When someone "bows" before a person or thing in religious devotion, he expresses religious worship and respect toward that person or thing. When someone "worships" a person or thing, it means that "he serves" that person or thing. He is a "servant" !

According to the above, God YHWH does not allow His people to "bend the knee" or to "bow out of religious devotion", to "worship", or "to serve", any other god except Him alone. He is a jealous God and He exacts this exclusive devotion !

When Daniel, the prophet, had a vision regarding the "son of man", Jesus in the flesh, he wrote:

"... And behold, one like the Son of man came with the clouds of the heavens. And He came to the Ancient of Days. And they brought Him near before Him. And dominion was given to Him, and glory, and a Kingdom, that all peoples, nations, and languages should serve Him".   (Daniel 7 : 13, 14)

We see that while God had forbidden the worship of others, this passage states that all the nations, the peoples and the languages, will worship (serve) Jesus !

Although in Isaiah 45:22, 23 God says: "Turn to Me and be saved, all the ends of the earth; for I am God, and there is no other. I have sworn by Myself, the word has gone out of My mouth in righteousness, and shall not return, that to Me every knee shall bow, every tongue shall swear", in the letter to

Philippians, chapter 2 : 10, 11, Paul says:

"at the name of Jesus every knee should bow, of those of Heaven, and those of earth, and those under the earth; and every tongue should confess that Jesus Christ is Lord, to the glory of God the Father." ! !

In other words, while in the Old Testament, God says that "there is no other God beside Me", and He swears by Himself that "every knee" will bow to Him, in the New Testament we read that "every knee" will bow to Jesus ! !

In the letter to the Hebrews, chapter 1 : 6, we read about Jesus:

"And let all the angels of God worship Him" ! !

PLEASE NOTE: The Greek word for "worship" (ΠΡΟΣΚΥΝΩ) found in the above verse is the same word for "worship" found in Revelation 22 : 9.

In Matt. 14:33, we read that the disciples of Jesus who were "... with Him in the boat, fell before Him and worshipped Him."

If Jesus were not "fully God" and "God by nature", equal to the Father and one of the true

Godhead YHWH, then, YHWH Himself would not have allowed others to worship Him.

The priests of the true God YHWH, worship or serve only Him. They are forbidden to be priests of "angels" or of "other gods". But when we read Revelation 20 : 6, we see that those who will take part in the first resurrection, **will be priests of God and of Christ !**

> Therefore, since God YHWH allows His priests to also be priests of Christ, since YHWH allows them to worship Jesus, then, beyond any doubt, Jesus is fully God, God by nature, and worthy to receive worship !

The first Christians, who believed that Jesus is God, and God's Son, were happy to worship Him. Let us examine the writings of Polycarp and Justin.

Polycarp, lived from 65 to 155/6 A.D. He became a Christian at an early age, and later a disciple of the apostle John. He was appointed by John to the position of Bishop over the church in Asia. The following words are taken from a letter written to the churches about his death:

"And Polycarp answered: Eighty - six years have I served Him, and He has never done me any harm. How could I blaspheme my King and my Savior?"

He also said, ". . . <u>Him we worship because He is the Son of God</u>." (Martyrdom of Polycarp, Chapter 17, Verse 10,  from the Greek text.)


Justin, lived from 95 to 165 A.D. He was a Gentile and became a Christian in his mature years. He became one of the greatest defenders of the Christian faith. He died as a martyr.

In Justin's writings, Jesus is repeatedly called God, and said to be the object of worship. Speaking about those who are Christians by name only, Justin, in  his "Dialogue with Trypho" said that they are ". . . atheists, impious, unrighteous, and sinful, and confessors of Jesus in name only, <u>instead of worshippers of Him</u>". (Chapter 35)


In the above book, he also wrote  regarding Christ, that  "<u>He deserves to be worshipped as God and as Christ</u>." !

In his  "Apology", he wrote:
"... Him ... the word of God together with God <u>we worship and love</u>."   (from the Greek text).

Therefore, we see that the first Christians acknowledged that Jesus is One of the true Godhead YHWH, and they worshipped Him even if it would lead to death.

The prophecy recorded in Isaiah 40 : 3 states:
"The voice of him who cries in the wilderness: Prepare the way of Jehovah; make straight in the desert a highway for our God." !

Whose way did John the baptist prepare? **Accord-ing to the above prophecy, he prepared the way of our God. ! !**

In the prophecy of Malachi 3 : 1, we hear the YHWH of hosts saying:
"Behold, I am sending My messenger, and he will clear the way before Me." ! !

Who came to the earth?  Whose way did John the baptist clear? **According to the above, he cleared the way of YHWH of Hosts.** (also read Zechariah 14 : 4)

Thus, once again, we see the perfect unity of YHWH the Father, with YHWH the Son, the unity of the one true God ! !

Beyond any doubt then, our Lord, Jesus Christ, the Son of the Living God, is God by Nature and should be worshipped.

# EPILOGUE

(INCLUDING A FEW WORDS FOR JEHOVAH'S WITNESSES)

That which has moved me to write this book, is the sense of responsibility which I felt I had before God and my fellow man.

In the 25th Chapter of the Gospel of Matthew, our Lord Jesus told us the parable of the "talents". From this parable, we learn that our Lord is happy, when we use the "talents" He gave us for His glory.

In verse 15 it says that ". . . to one indeed he gave five talents, and to another two, and to another, one -- to each according to his ability . . ."

As the story unfolds, we see that the slave who received the five talents from the lord, used them, and gained for the lord, five more.

The second slave, who received the two talents, used them and gained two more for his lord.

Both the first and second slaves made their lord happy.

The third slave received only one talent; instead of using it so he could make some profit for the lord, he hid it in the earth. When his lord came back, the third slave returned to him the one talent that his lord had given him !

In verses 26 and 27, we hear the lord saying to the third slave: "... Evil and slothful slave ! ... you ought to have put my silver to the bankers; and coming, I would have received my own with interest." !

When I saw the grandeur of the glory of Jesus Christ, my Lord, I considered this knowledge to be like a "talent" which He gave to me. Not wanting to be like the third slave, and to hide it in me, that is, in this earthly vessel in which I dwell, I considered it to be my responsibility to present this subject, to the best of my ability. I did this hoping that some day, someone will benefit, and in the joy of his knowledge of the Lord, he will give glory to Him who gives the "talents" ! I am referring to the joy which is born in a man, when he understands the glory of his Saviour God.

I did not always have this joy. I was born a Witness of Jehovah, and the organization to which I belonged deprived me of this joy. I was taught that Jesus is some "other god", less than the Father. They turned me, without my becoming aware of it, into a polytheist, believing in two

Gods:

  a)  in the Almighty Father, and

  b)  in the "mighty", but <u>not Almighty Son</u> -- as if there is something that the Lord Jesus is unable to do ! WHAT A SHAME !

> They did not help me to understand that when Jesus was saying certain words, which showed that He was lower than the Father, it was during the short period of time, in which He had humbled Himself and had taken on Himself the form of men. During that time, He had taken upon Himself a form lower than even the angels.

When He said: "All authority in Heaven and on earth was given to Me" (Matt. 28 : 18), it did not mean that He never had this authority before He became a man. It meant that the Father God gave "All authority" to the "man Jesus Christ", who now holds the position of the mediator between God and men !

"The man Jesus", asked His heavenly Father to give Him the glory which He (the "Word") had in Heaven, before the world was made!   (John 17 : 5)

Not having the Bible as the basis of their teaching, "they" brought me to the point of believing that the "Word", the Creator God, without Whom nothing was created, is Himself a creature ! !   What darkness !

They used the words of Colossians 1 : 16, where, (according to their NWT), it says about Jesus:
". . . all [other] things have been created through Him and for Him",  and they said:
"You see ?  Here it says 'through Him' all 'other' things have been created. These words mean that God created all things 'through' Jesus !  Therefore, Jesus is not God !"

PLEASE NOTE: The word "other" does not exist in the original Greek text. The Jehovah's Witnesses have added this word to their Bible translation to help support their theory that God created Jesus first and then <u>through Him,</u> all "other" things were created ! God is against those who add to His word. (Rev. 22 : 18)
Using the above reasoning, they present Jesus as a creature and as the "medium", "through" whom God created. Can they be correct? Is the Greek grammar able to help us determine whether Col. 1 : 16 says that Jesus is the "medium" only "through" whom someone else created or whether He is <u>the cause and the medium</u> of creation?  Let us study the text directly

from the original Greek. The exact wording from the Greek is: "In Him all things were created . . . all things were created 'ΔΙ' ΑΥΤΟΥ' (by Him) and for Him."

The Greek word "ΔΙΑ" (ΔΙ' for short) in the above text is a preposition. It has many different meanings depending on whether it is used for a place, for distance, for time, for a person etc. Some of the meanings are: for, by, with, about, through, etc. e.g. ΔΙΑ ΝΑ (in order to). ΔΙΑ ΒΙΟΥ (for life). ΔΙΑ ΤΟΥΤΟ (for this reason). ΔΙΑ ΠΛΟΙΟΥ (by boat). ΔΙΑ ΜΕΣΟΥ ΤΗΣ ΠΟΛΕΩΣ (through the city). Check Divrys Greek-English Dictionary, 1971, page 471, under the word "ΔΙΑ".

According to ΕΚΣΥΓΧΡΟΝΙΣΜΕΝΟΝ "1970", ΝΕΟΝ ΛΕΞΙΚΟΝ (ΔΗΜΗΤΡΑΚΟΥ), page 397, under the word "ΔΙΑ", no. 7, the grammar of the Greek language dictates that:

> when the word "ΔΙΑ" is used in regards to an act of a person, followed by the genitive case, it means that the person is the cause of this act --- NOT JUST THE MEDIUM !

When the word "ΔΙΑ" is followed by the word "ΜΕΣΩ" it means "through" and shows that the person is only the medium. The combination of both words makes the person to be "diamesos" --- intermediate or medium. (check the above Lexicon ΔΗΜΗΤΡΑΚΟΥ, page 409, under the word "ΔΙΑΜΕΣΟΣ").

In Col. 1 : 16 <u>we do not find</u> the word "ΜΕΣΩ" after the word "ΔΙΑ"; it does NOT say "... ΔΙΑ ΜΕΣΩ ΑΥΤΟΥ ...". Instead, we see that the word "ΔΙΑ" is followed by the word "ΑΥΤΟΥ" (Him) which is in the genitive case. When a Greek word is in the genitive case, and is translated into English, it should receive in front of it the words "of the" or "of". Therefore, the expression "ΔΙ' ΑΥΤΟΥ" should literally be translated as "by of the Him" or "by of Him". Although "all things were created by of Him" sounds strange, it makes an irrefutable point --- it makes the person (Him) to be the Cause, the Author of creation.

"In Him all things were created", means that Jesus is the AUTHOR, THE ONE WHO CONCEIVED IN HIS WISDOM the pattern of all things which ". . . were created by Him and for Him" ! That makes Jesus THE DESIGNER AND THE BUILDER who created all things for Himself. He is the Creator

**G o d .** Also check Romans 11 : 36 where the above words "ΔIA AYTOY", meaning "by Him", are used for God. There, it states:

"O the depth of the riches and of the wisdom and the knowledge of God . . . Because of Him, and by Him (ΔI' AYTOY) and to Him are all things" !!

The above scriptures have one target: the One who created all things and for whom all things were created. Thus, we clearly see that all things were created by the Father and by the Son, for the Father and for the Son. Therefore, the Father is God and the Son is God.

The JW's make another mistake by saying that Jesus, in His prehuman nature, was an angel; they preach that Jesus is Michael the archangel -- without having any scriptures to prove this claim !

Who is Michael? What is his nature? Does the Bible say anywhere that Michael is God?

NO ! It does not mention anywhere that Michael is God ! There is not one verse which says that the form, the likeness or the nature of Michael was or is Divine, as it does about Jesus ! !

The authority of Michael is not like the authority of Jesus ! Michael's authority is less than the authority of the Devil. This fact is supported by the words of the apostle Jude: "But Michael, the archangel, when contending with the Devil, he argued about the body of Moses -- he dared not bring a judgement of blasphemy, but said, Let the Lord rebuke you !" (ver. 9).

However, Jesus, "the Word", "by", or "through" Whom all things (including the Devil) were created, showed on many occasions that He had greater power than Satan and his demons; He even gave this authority to His disciples, to have authority in His Name over all the power of the Enemy.   (Luke 9 : 1; 4:36; 10 : 17-20)

From the  above scriptures, we see that while Michael did not dare to rebuke Satan, Jesus, even at the time when He emptied Himself and became flesh, had authority over all the power of the enemy ! (Luke 10 : 17 - 20).   Rightfully, Jesus has greater authority than the Devil, because He, the "Word", is the Creator, while the Devil is a creature !    (John 1:1-3; Ezek. 28:11-19).

In addition, Jesus is the only begotten Son of God ---- the only born of the Father.  Thus, <u>Jesus is unique in the whole universe. There is no one else like Him</u>. On the other hand, Michael is not unique. He is "one" of  many like him. This is stated in Daniel 10 : 13: ". . . But, lo,  <u>Michael, "one  of  the  first  rulers"</u>, came to help me . . ." !

The words, "one of" show that Michael is not unique, and that there are more like him ! !

Michael has been appointed to look after the righteous people of God; he stands for the sons of Israel, and he is a leader of a group of angels (this is why he is called archangel). Also, he is the one whom God used to make war with Satan and his angels, and to cast them down to the earth. (Daniel 12:1; Revelation 12:7-9).

Since Michael is an archangel, <u>his nature is that of a created angel --- not that of the uncreated God</u> !

From the above scriptures, which are the only ones referring to the person of the archangel Michael, we see that he was not Jesus. Nowhere do we find Michael holding a "position", a "title", or an "office", that belongs to Jesus. For this reason, it is clear that Jesus is not and never was Michael !

Every knee will not bow in the name of Michael, but in the name of Jesus, because Jesus is God by nature --- not an angel !

**God did not subject the coming world to angels** (Hebrews 2:5), but placed all things under the feet of Jesus who created them, because "for Him" all things were made. (Col. 1:16; Rom. 11: 33-36; Heb. 2 : 10)

Michael is not one of the Godhead YHWH who created all things. The fullness of the uncreated Godhead <u>does not</u> dwell in Michael !

If our Saviour is not the God of Israel, the One who said, "I, I am YHWH; and there is no Saviour besides Me", (Isaiah 43:11), then, all of us owe our lives to the archangel Michael ! Can it be that the name "Michael" means YHWH the Saviour"? NO ! But the name "Jesus" does !

Now, how was it possible that I did not understand all these points and the glory of Jesus, all the years I was a Witness of Jehovah? The answer is simple. Jesus said,"Ask, and it will be given to you;". (Matt. 7:7). <u>I had not asked God to reveal His Son to me</u>, because I believed (like every other Witness of Jehovah), that our organization had the full truth about the person of our Lord !

The apostle Paul said that God revealed His Son to him. He wrote: "But when God was pleased, He having separated me from my mother's womb, . . . <u>to</u>

reveal His Son in me, that I might preach Him among the nations;" ! (Gal. 1 : 15, 16)

Why is it necessary for God to reveal Jesus to us? Because, ". . . no one knows the Son except the Father" (Matt. 11 : 27), and "No one is able to come to Me unless the Father . . . draws him;". (John 6 : 44)

Another reason for the Father to be involved in order for us to understand Jesus and His glory, is that ". . . the god of this age (Satan), has blinded the thoughts of the unbelieving, so that the brightness of the gospel of the glory of Christ, who is the image of God, should not dawn on them . . . Because God, who said the light to shine out of darkness, has shone in our hearts, to give the light of the knowledge of the glory of God in the face of Jesus Christ." (2 Cor. 4:4 - 6 -- from the Greek)

Why did Satan blind the thoughts of men, so that the brightness of the gospel of the glory of Christ, who is the image of God, should not dawn on them? What would Satan have to gain by blinding the unbelieving?

Here is the way I see it:

When we read from the book of Isaiah, chapter 14, and verses 12 to 14, we see that Satan (Lucifer or shining star), was saying in his heart: ". . . I will go up to the heavens; I will raise my throne above the

stars of God, and I will sit in the mount of meeting,
. . . I will be compared to the Most High." !

From these words, we see that Satan wanted to be
like the Most High !  However, because he is a creature,
it is impossible for him to be *by nature* like the Most
High; thus, he tried to lower the "Word",  his Creator,
in the thoughts of men and to present Him as a part of
the creation !  In other words, in order to satisfy his
pride, (that is, to be compared to the Most High), he
tried to lower, in the minds of men,  the nature of his
Creator, Jesus, to the level of a created being like
himself !

The religious leaders of certain sects,  serving the
prideful motives of Satan, have removed from the
thoughts of men  the glory of the Lord Jesus, by
teaching them that He, the Creator Jesus, and the
creature Satan, are brothers !

I repeat,  Jesus is the only begotten Son of God,
which means the only born of God  -- He is unique.
Satan was created -- he is a creature.  JESUS AND Satan
ARE NOT BROTHERS BY NATURE ! !  (John 1:18;
3:16; Ezek. 28:13, 15)

Another point the Witnesses use in order to prove

that Jesus is not God by nature, (because according to them only the Father is God by nature), is that Satan tested Jesus in the desert, at the beginning of His earthly ministry.

Because Satan said to Jesus, "All these things I will give you if you fall down and do an act of worship to me" (NWT), the Witnesses maintain that Satan was trying to cause Jesus to be disloyal to God. They say, "if Jesus were God, could God rebel against himself? The temptation of Jesus would make sense only if he was, not God, but a separate individual who had his own free will, one who could be disloyal to God."

They use Deuteronomy 32 : 4, where it says of God, "Perfect is his activity . . . A God of faithfulness, . . . righteous and upright is he.", and they say that it is unimaginable that God could sin and be disloyal to himself. <u>So, they say, if Jesus had been God, he could not have been tempted</u>. (Read their publication, "SHOULD YOU BELIEVE IN THE TRINITY?" page 14, subtitle "COULD GOD BE TEMPTED?")

Their conclusion is incorrect. It shows that they have failed to understand the Godhead. They have also failed to see the reason Jesus came to the earth,

in what form He came, and who wanted to test Him --
God or Satan?

All of us will agree that Jesus came to the earth to
be sacrificed for the sins of the world, that whosoever
believes in Him will have eternal life. This is not all
the Christ did for us. He also gave us freedom from
bondage and from the works which religion imposed
upon the human race, giving the false hope that men
could please God and receive eternal life through
works !

Christ also made it possible for believers to become
sons of God ! **He made us a new creation.**
(2 Cor. 5:17;  Gal. 6:15;  Col. 3:10;  Eph. 4:24)

The old creation with the first Adam, brought sin
and death to the human race. The new creation, of the
last Adam, Jesus Christ, brought freedom from sin and
death.

When God made the old creation, it was <u>His</u>
purpose to test Adam. <u>He allowed</u> Satan to test Adam
and he fell.  With the first coming of our Lord Jesus,
we saw <u>the beginning of a new creation</u>. The "Word",
the Creator Himself,  became flesh in order to start this
new creation, because, all things came into being
through Him and without Him not even one thing

came into being that has come into being !     (John 1 :
1 - 3)

Jesus, the One who is the "Author" of the creation
of God, became the "firstborn" or the "head" of the
new creation. (Rev. 3:14; Col. 1: 9 - 20.  See pages 43,
44).  We,  the  believers,  are  part  of  this  "NEW
CREATION".

Is this new creation superior to the old?  Would
the new creation prove to be stronger  than  the  old?
Could  it  stand  steadfast under the temptations of
Satan?

God is the fountain of life. Whatever comes out of
God is living. Only life can come out of life, as only
light can come out of light. The "Word" of God is not
a dead sound, for the word of God is living,  working
powerfully, and able to judge the thoughts and the
intentions of the heart. There is no creature unrevealed
before Him; but all things are naked and laid open to
Him to whom we have to give account !  (Heb. 4 : 12,
13)

Don't the above words prove that the "Word" is
God?  And yet, God, the "Word", became flesh, to live
among us as a man. The  "Word"  did  not come to the

earth to live as God, but as a man. It was God's purpose -- not Satan's -- to test <u>the man</u> Jesus. The Holy Spirit led Jesus to the desert to be tested by Satan. (Matthew 4:1 -- <u>NESTLE-ALAND</u> GREEK TEXT)

As a man, He became hungry and the nature of His Father, which is in Him (John 14 : 10, 11), could easily have turned the stones into bread so He could eat; but He did not do that because He had to suffer the pains of hunger as a man, trusting God.

As a man, He subjected Himself to the law.

As a man, not as God, He learned (experi - enced) obedience.

As a man -- not as God, Satan tried to tempt Him in all things.

As a man, He died on the cross.

As a man, He was buried.

As a man, He was raised and glorified.

As a man, He became the mediator between God and men, and as the mediator, He sits at the right hand of the Father until all things are made new. Therefore, the reasoning of the Jehovah's Witnesses is incorrect because <u>Satan did not try to tempt God the "Word" in the desert, but the man Jesus</u>, the "beginning", or the "head" of the new creation. And Jesus proved that this new creation has the power to say "NO" to Satan and to sin (John 14 : 30). Praise God, because greater is He who is in us, than he who is in the world, and therefore, He has given us the power to say "NO" to Satan and to sin (1 John 4:4).

Dear Reader, if at the present time, you are in the position where I once was, and you do not know Jesus and His glory, ask the Father to reveal Him to you, and He will. He answered my prayer; He will also answer yours. The Lord Jesus said, *". . . Ask, and it will be given to you. Seek, and you will find; knock, and it will be opened to you. For everyone asking, receives, and the one seeking finds; and to the one knocking, it will be opened."*   (Luke 11 : 9 - 13)

> Consider, when you look at yourself in the mirror, you are looking at your image --- not someone else's. When you look at your image, you are looking at yourself ! Jesus is the image of the invisible God ! Those who saw Jesus, when He was on earth, saw God. (2 Cor. 4:4; Col. 1:15; 1 Cor. 13:12)

May God give you the joy of the understanding which He gave me.

At this point, I feel that this book would be incomplete if I do not include my experience as to how God revealed to me the deity of the Lord Jesus. Before I do this, I would like to bring to your attention certain scriptures, (which, perhaps, you have not paid attention to, if you are a Witness of Jehovah), because I know the teaching of the Watchtower Society on this subject, and I understand your feelings and fears. Allow me to proceed step by step with questions and answers.

Do you believe that we are living in the last days of this system of things?

I know your answer is YES.

What does the prophecy of Joel say that Jehovah will do before the coming of the great and awesome day of Jehovah?

Let us read from Joel 2 : 27 - 31:

"And you shall know that I (am) in Israel's midst, and that I (am) Jehovah your God, and none else; and my people shall not be ashamed forever.

And it shall be afterward, I will pour out My Spirit on all flesh. And your sons and your daughters shall prophesy; your old men shall dream dreams, your young men shall see visions . . . before the coming of the great and awesome day of Jehovah."

From the above, we see that it is God - not Satan - the One who pours His Spirit on all flesh in order for some to prophesy, others to dream dreams and others to see visions before the coming of the awesome day of Jehovah.

The first Christians experienced that which was spoken by the prophet Joel on the day of Pentecost. As we read from the book of Acts, we see that the Spirit of God continued to be poured upon the faithful even after the day of Pentecost.

> Consider, there is not one scripture which says that the pouring out of the Holy Spirit and the gifts which He would give to men would stop with the death of the apostles --- not one verse !

Your organization, and some others, who have not experienced this wonderful gift, make this claim. They are preventing "their" people, "their" members, from experiencing this beautiful personal relationship with God.

Another reason they preach the above "demonic" teaching (that all the gifts of the Spirit have stopped with the death of the apostles), is to have exclusive authority, full control, over "their" people. They want

their followers to be dependent on "them" for
guidance rather than training them to depend on the
Holy Spirit.  (John 16:13)

    They say that the following diagram represents the
route which the "light of the truth" follows to reach
the individual:

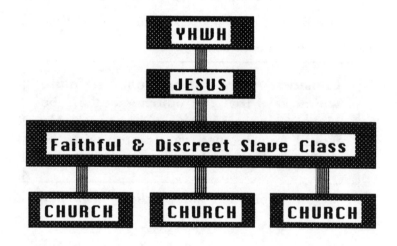

    The Witnesses claim that the "light of the truth"
comes from YHWH, who gives it to Jesus, who gives it
to the "Faithful and Discreet Slave Class", who,
through the publications of the Watchtower Society,
give it to "their" Churches.

They enforce ruthlessly the teaching that they are the "ONLY" channel of God's truth; they teach that ONLY THROUGH THEM, (the faithful and discreet slave "class"), will God speak to His people.

> BE CAREFUL: Domination is the main characteristic of all false cults.

These have brought upon their members, whom they have turned into fanatics, physical and spiritual death. They make their members believe that they must suffer persecution for the name of God, while in reality they suffer persecution for the name of their organization.

> BE CAREFUL especially of those cults which "grab" the place of Jesus. He said, "I am the truth", yet these organizations claim that they are "the truth" !

Since Jesus is "the truth" (John 14 : 6), then His words are true. He said, "And I will ask the Father, and He shall give you another Comforter, (the Spirit of truth), that he may abide with you forever" -- not just till the death of the apostles !

The Holy Spirit dwells in the believers and He guides them into all truth. (John 16 : 13; 1 Cor. 3 : 16)

Jesus also said, "the Spirit of truth, which the

world cannot receive, because it sees Him not, neither knows Him; but you know Him, for He abides with you and shall be in you." (John 14 : 17)

The true believers are not part of "the world". The world cannot receive the Holy Spirit. The true believers are the temple of God and the Holy Spirit dwells in them ! (Gal. 3 : 26 - 29; John 14 : 17). DON'T KEEP THE HOLY SPIRIT OUT OF YOUR LIFE ! !

Again, Jesus said, ". . . the Comforter, the Holy Spirit, which the Father will send in my name, He shall teach you all things, and bring all things to your remembrance, whatsoever I have said to you." Jesus did not say that an "organization" shall teach you all things ! (John 14 : 26)

> The word "Organization", and the expressions "Governing Body" and "Faithful and Discreet Slave Class", as such, do not exist in the Bible !

The Scriptures teach us that the "Head" of every man or the "Head" of the church is Christ (Eph. 5:23; 1 Cor. 11:3). Nowhere in the Bible does it state that the "Head" of every man or the "Head" of the church should be an "organization" or the "Governing body" of some publishing house, or a "class" of men who call themselves "The Faithful and Discreet Slave" !

According to the words of our Lord Jesus, the
Christian life we lead will prove if we are faithful,
discreet, good, faithful stewards or wicked, slothful
and useless servants ! (Matt. 24 : 45, 50; 25 : 21, 23,
26, 30; Luke 12 : 42)

> The "faithful and discreet slave
> class" of the Watchtower Society, has
> proven to be a false prophet, because
> over the last one hundred years or
> so, it has falsely prophesied many
> times. This record, by itself,
> is already enough to remove from
> this "class" the right to be the
> "only channel" of God's truths to
> the faithful. (see Appendix E, p.192)

Jesus would never appoint a false prophet over all
His belongings ! (Matt. 24 : 47) In the law of the Old
Testament, the will of God was that a false prophet
ought to be killed by His people -- not to be exalted as
leader ! (Deut. 18 : 20) Today, we Christians, live
under the law of the New Testament -- the law of love.
The law of love forbids us to kill false prophets; we try
to reach out to them with love, but we do not follow
them.

Our Lord Jesus forewarned us that such false

prophets would come before the end of this age, and He told us <u>not to believe them</u>: "Then if any man shall say unto you, Lo, here is Christ, or there; believe not." (Matt. 24 : 23)

In verse 24, Jesus says, "False Christs", which means "false anointed ones", and false prophets will arise, and will try to deceive, if it were possible, the very elect. In verse 26, He says, ". . . if they (the false prophets and the false anointed ones) shall say unto you, Behold, He is in the desert; go not forth: behold, He is in the secret chambers; (of their organization?), believe (it) not."

Finally, in verse 27, our Lord said, "For as the lightning comes out of the east, and appears as far as the west; so shall also be the presence of the Son of man."

The "faithful and discreet slave class" of the organization of Jehovah's Witnesses, preach that <u>only the true and faithful Witnesses of Jehovah "saw" the newly arrived Lord in 1914 A.D., with their mind's eyes</u> ! Therefore, in this way they say, "Here is Christ" since 1914 A.D. They fit exactly into the category of verses 23 and 26. By saying only they saw Jesus with the eyes of their minds and not with their physical eyes, they are contradicted by the words of Revelation 1 : 7, where it says:

"Behold, He comes with the clouds, and <u>every eye shall see Him, . . ."</u>! <u>Even the eyes of His enemies</u> ! Here, it does not mention "mind's eyes" !

From the above, we clearly see that the "faithful and discreet slave class" of Jehovah's Witnesses cannot be the only channel of God's truth, therefore, they cannot guide us into all truth !

> Only the Holy Spirit guides us to the Truth, because only He receives from Jesus and reveals Him to every believer. (John 16:12-15)

The Scripture which the faithful and discreet slave class use, in order to mislead you and to bring you to the point of believing that the outpouring of the Holy Spirit, with the operation of the gifts has stopped since the death of the apostles, is 1 Cor. 13 : 8-13. There it reads:

"Love never fails. But if there are prophecies, they will be abolished; if tongues, they shall cease; <u>if knowledge, it will be abolished</u>; for we know in part, and we prophesy in part; but when the perfect (thing) comes, then that which is in part will be caused to cease.

When I was an infant, I spoke as an infant, I thought as an infant, I reasoned as an infant. But when I became a man, I did away with the things of the infant. For now we see through a mirror in dimness, <u>but then face to face</u>. Now I know in part, but then I will fully know even as I also was fully known. And now faith, hope, and love, these three (things) remain; but the greatest of these is love."

Here, in chapter 13, the apostle Paul speaks of the gifts of the Spirit, about which he started talking in chapter 12. He compares those with "love", saying that if someone has the gift of speaking in tongues or if he has the gift of prophecy or the gift to know all the mysteries, and if he has all the knowledge, if he does not have love, he is nothing. (verse 2)

In verses 4 - 7, he says how love treats others: "Love has patience, is kind; love is not envious; . . . does not behave indecently . . .",  etc.

In verses 8 - 13, he writes that while all the other

gifts of the Spirit, like the prophecies, the languages and the knowledge, someday will cease, "love", he says, "never fails", is eternal, and greater than faith and hope.

In verse 10, the apostle says that the gifts of the Spirit will cease "when the perfect comes". **He does not say that the gifts will cease at the death of the apostles!** Neither does he say that the "perfect" will come "when the Holy Bible will be completed as a book", as some say.

When will the "perfect" come? When will the gifts cease?

In verse 12, he says, "For now we see through a mirror in dimness, <u>but then face to face,</u> Now, I know in part, but then I will fully know even as I also was fully known."

Where he writes the word "<u>then</u>", he means "<u>when the perfect comes</u>"; "<u>then</u>" <u>we will see</u> "<u>face to face</u>".

Whom will we see "face to face"? What was the apostle Paul seeing as through a mirror? Paul writes in 2 Cor. 3 : 18: "... we all with our face having been unveiled, are beholding the glory of the Lord in a mirror . . ."    (From the Greek)

John, the disciple of Christ, wrote:

"Beloved, now we are the children of God, and it was not yet revealed what we shall be. But we know that <u>when He is revealed</u>, we shall be like Him, because <u>we shall see Him as He is</u>." !   (1 John 3 : 2)

In Revelation 22 : 1 - 4, we see that when all things become perfect, "and every curse will no longer be", the servants of God will serve Him, and they "will see His face;" !

<u>"Then"</u>, <u>when the perfect comes, we will see Him face to face</u> ! "Then", the gifts of the Spirit, like the prophecies, the languages, the gift of healing, etc. will cease.

> "Then", the need for these gifts will not be there, because we will be with the Lord and we will be seeing His glory and His face forever.

Only "love" will remain forever, because the eternal God is love   (1 John 4:8).

Therefore, since the "perfect" has not yet come, all the gifts and operations of the Holy Spirit should still be among us, having been given to the different members of the body of Christ for their common benefit. (1 Cor., Chapter 12)

Prophecies and languages are not the only gifts of the Spirit. The gifts also include the word of wisdom, knowledge, faith, healings, the discerning of spirits, visions, dreams, and revelations. (Acts 16 : 9; 10 : 3 - 20; 9 : 10; 1 Cor. 12 : 1 - 11; Joel 2 : 28-31).

All the gifts of the Spirit continue to operate in the church today. The gifts, which the believers in Christ displayed from the day of Pentecost onwards, were the visual proof that the promised Helper, the Spirit of truth, had arrived to be with them --- not just until the death of the apostles, as some say, but "forever" as Jesus said:

"And I will ask the Father, and he will give you another Counselor to be with you forever." (John 14:16 --- NIV)

If anyone believes that the gifts of the Spirit ceased with the death of the apostles, he actually believes that the Lord Jesus Christ did not keep his promise when He said "forever" ! The presence of the Holy Spirit is known by the presence of His gifts. The absence of the gifts means the absence of the Holy Spirit. It is not difficult to imagine the spiritual condition of a body of believers in which the Spirit is not present. The "Truth" and freedom will not be there --- neither will the "joy" and the rest of the fruit of the Spirit. (2 Cor. 3:17; Gal. 5:22)

Since the Holy Spirit is with us today, all His gifts must be with us. These gifts will help the believers in their Christian walk until the "perfect" comes, and the "Kingdom of God", which all of us are waiting for, is established.

The Bible speaks in many places about "dreams" and "visions". It says that dreams are one of the ways in which God speaks to man. Open your Bible to the book of Job, chapter 33 and verses 14 - 17. There it says:

*"For God speaks once, And twice -- though one does not regard it. In a dream, a vision of the night, when deep sleep falls upon men, during slumbers upon the bed. It is then that he uncovers the ear of men, And on exhortation to them he puts his seal, to turn aside a man from his deed, And that he may cover pride itself from an able-bodied man." !*
*(NWT)*

Now, open your Bible to the book of Numbers, chapter 12 and verse 6. There, God says:

"... Hear my words, please. *If there came to be*

*a prophet of yours for Jehovah, it would be in a vision I would make myself known to him.  In a dream I would speak to him." !*

The Bible describes a multitude of cases in which God or an angel of God, appeared to men in dreams and He spoke to them. Examine some of them:

```
Genesis    20:3
   "       31:10,11,24
Matthew    1:20
   "       2:12,13,19,22
   "       27:19
Daniel     7:1
   "       8:18
```

That very thing happened to me. When I asked God Jehovah, in the name of our Lord Jesus Christ, to help me understand who Jesus is, whether He is some "angel", outside the uncreated Godhead YHWH, or "one" of the true Godhead YHWH, our Lord gave me a dream, which was the beginning of my understanding:

"I was looking at the sea. In the sea, I saw a mountain which was like an island.  The mountain had the shape of a triangle with  equal  sides.  It was made out of solid rock; there were no trees on it nor any grass. This mountain was unique. There was no other mountain or island beside it.

In the lower part of the mountain, there was a cave. Standing in front of this cave, I saw two tall men with white hair and white beards. The two looked exactly the same except that one appeared to be somewhat younger than the other. The one was the exact image of the other. They looked so much alike that if I had seen one without the other, I would not have been able to tell which one I was looking at.

Both of them wore coveralls. Suddenly, the slightly older one left, and the younger one remained. He looked into my eyes and smiled with love and compassion."

With this dream, the Paraclete, the Holy Spirit, reminded me of the following scriptures:

DANIEL 7 : 9  ". . . and  the Ancient of Days sat down
           . . . and  the hair  of his head was like clean
           wool. His   throne   was  flames   of  fire;"
           (NWT)

REV. 1 : 13, 14    ". . . I saw . . . someone like a son of man . . . his head and his hair were white as white wool, as snow . . ." (NWT)

COL. 1 : 15    "He (Jesus)* is the image of the invisible God . . ." (NWT)

JOHN 5 : 17, 18    "But he (Jesus)* answered them: 'My Father has kept working until now, and I keep working.' On this account, indeed the Jews began seeking all the more to kill him because not only was he breaking the Sabbath but he was also calling God his own Father, making himself equal to God," (NWT)

PHIL. 2 : 5 - 8 ". . . Christ Jesus, who subsisting in the form of God, thought it not robbery to be equal with God." (from the Greek text)

---

PLEASE NOTE: Based on the above quotation, how many do you know who are subsisting in the form of God? --- not in "a god's form", not in an "angel's form", but in God's form !

---

* The name (Jesus) has been inserted by the author.

With this dream and with the above verses, I began to understand the close relationship that exists between the Son and the Father, but my knowledge of the Son was still incomplete. As a Witness of Jehovah, I knew of the Father and of the Son, but I had been "taught" that there was a great distance between them. But now, with this dream, the Lord picked me up from where my understanding was, and helped me to see how close the Father and the Son are.

Another day as I was alone meditating on this close relationship that exists between the Father and the Son, the day of the creation came to my mind.

In Genesis 1 : 3, God said, "Let light be --- and there was light." The main point of this verse is that God SAID, "Let light be"! For all the things which God created, He created them by the word He spoke. All things were made by the WORD of God. His WORD made all things; and the WORD became flesh and tabernacled among us, and we beheld His glory ! (John 1 : 14)

John's simple words began to echo in my mind:

"and the WORD became flesh",

"and the WORD became flesh",

"and the WORD became flesh" !

And we saw the "Word", the creative power and authority of God, in the face of Jesus Christ !

Suddenly, my soul and spirit were filled with satisfaction . . . THE WORD OF GOD (John 1:1),
the absolute creative power of God (John 1:3),
the absolute wisdom of God (1 Cor. 1:24,30),
the absolute image of God (Col. 1:15),
the expression of God's love (John 3:16),
the absolute light of God (John 1:9),
the Creator of the ages (Hebrews 1:2),
the radiance, the shining splendour of God's glory
(Heb. 1:3),
the express image of God's essence (Heb.1:3),
THE PANTOKPATOR OR ALMIGHTY, the One who holds all things with the word of His power (Heb. 1:3), BECAME FLESH ! ! Thus, we came to know God and His glory, in the face of Jesus Christ (2 Cor. 4:6; John 14:7-9) !

How could I have believed for all those years that:
the "Word" of God was a created angel?
the absolute creative power of God was a created angel?
the absolute wisdom of God which designed all things

within Himself was a created angel?

the absolute image of God was a created angel?

the expression of God's love was a created angel?

the absolute light of God was a created angel?

the Creator of the Ages, who was in existence before them was a created angel?

the radiance, the shining splendour of God's glory, was a created angel?

the express image of God's essence was a created angel?

the One "who holds all things with the word of His power", the Pantokrator (the Omnipotent God) was a created angel?

Jesus, please forgive me for my ignorance.


On another morning, I was home alone, sitting in the living-room, praying and magnifying God.

It was about eleven o'clock. Suddenly, I saw in front of me a wonderful vision:

"I saw a great white fire. This fire was nothing like the fires I had seen in my life. It was not burning anything! It did not have the red and orange colors of an earthly fire, neither did it have any smoke. It was a white fire; it had the height of a tall person, and it was radiating a pure, white light !

The fire consisted of many white and living flames; the flames were intertwining, one flame embracing the other in an upward spiral. This white, bright fire was slowly and gracefully rotating around itself.

On the upper part of this fire, I saw the face of Jesus ! It was the face of the man Jesus, the man who had suffered pain. As the fire rotated, the face of the Lord Jesus disappeared at the rear of the fire; I could not see any other face, until the face of the Lord Jesus slowly appeared again at the other side of the fire." !

What a beautiful vision of God's glory ! What a beautiful understanding of the mystery of God and of Christ, of the mystery of the Godhead ! (Col. 2 : 2, 3)

The apostle Paul said that God dwells in unapproachable light, whom not one of men has seen or can see ! (1 Tim. 6 : 16) Again, Paul wrote, *"For it is the God who said, 'Let light shine out of darkness,' Who has shone in our hearts to give the light of the knowledge of the glory of God in the face of Christ".* (2 Cor. 4 : 6)

On another night, the Lord Jesus appeared again in my dream. I dreamt I was sitting in a chair. Jesus came close to me; He also sat in a chair, and looked at me, smiling.

"Lord", I said, "as I understand You now, You represented the Father <u>in full</u> when You were on earth. In other words, those who saw You, saw the Father" !

"Yes", He answered smiling, "this is what <u>We</u> want you to understand." !

My soul glorifies the Lord for the mercy He showed me, an imperfect man. There is nothing in this world of greater value, than for a man to know his Creator.

This is my treasure: that I came to know Him, because He was known to me (as in a mirror), and because I was known by Him, the good and humble

God. The glory belongs to Him, now and forever. (1 Peter 4 : 11; 2 Peter 3 : 18)

I hope that you will come to know Him also. Then, you will experience the height of the joy which fills His children for His glory !

# JESUS INVITES YOU !

Jesus said:

"Behold, I stand at the door and knock; if any man hears my voice and opens the door, I will go in to him, . . ." (Revelation 3 : 20)

From the above, we see that Jesus is good, polite and meek. He does not try to force anyone to open the "door" and to accept Him. "If" someone receives Him out of his own free will and opens the "door" of his heart, then Jesus comes to dwell inside him.

Jesus does not come into the heart alone. The Father, who is in the Son, comes in also. Jesus said, "... if a man loves me, he will keep my words; and my Father will love him, and we will come into him, and make our abode with him" (John 14:23). The Father and the Son dwell in us through the Holy Spirit. (Rom. 8:9-11)

The believer becomes the "temple of God". The apostle Paul said to the Corinthian Christians:

"Do you not know that you are the temple of God, and the Spirit of God dwells in you . . . the temple of God is holy, which you are." (1 Cor. 3:16,17)

When the Spirit of God indwells the believer, he is "born again". From this moment, the "born again" person has direct access to God through the Holy Spirit. At this moment, the believer becomes a child of the Most High God. (John 3:3-5;1:12,13; Rom.8:14-16)

Are you born again? Does Christ dwell in you? Are you saved?

Perhaps you have asked yourself:
What must I do to be saved? I am a sinner. How can my sins be forgiven? How can I become a child of God as others have? Is it possible that God will accept me into His family as well?

Dear friend, the Holy Scriptures give clear answers to your questions. You are absolutely right when you say that you are a sinner. All men are sinners. You are not an exception. The Bible says:

"for all sinned and come short of the glory of God". (Rom. 3:23)

Believe that God loves you.

"For God so loved the world that He gave His only-begotten Son, that everyone believing into Him should not perish, but have everlasting life. For God did not send His Son into the world that He might judge the world but the world might be saved through

Him." (John 3 : 16, 17)

It is because of God's love that we receive salvation. We do not have to work for it --- it's God's free gift to us !

"For by grace are ye saved through faith; and that not of yourselves; it is the gift of God; not of works, lest any man should boast. For we are his workmanship, created in Christ Jesus unto good works, which God hath before ordained that we should walk in them." (Eph. 2 : 8-10)

Take this moment to make the greatest decision of your life. Pray to God something like this:

"My God, thank you for sending Your Son to die for me. Please forgive me for my sins. Please reveal yourself to me and show me the way to serve you. Lead me to the Lord Jesus who is the truth and the life. Lord Jesus, I open the door of my heart. Please come in and be my Lord. Amen."

Now that you have asked our Heavenly Father to forgive your sins, rejoice because your sins are forgiven.

When the apostle Peter preached to Cornelius and his family about Jesus, he said to them that, "... through his name (Jesus') whosoever believeth in him shall receive remission of sins." (Acts 10:43)

While Peter was still talking to them, the Holy Spirit fell upon them. (verse 44)

When Peter saw that God accepted Cornelius and his household into His family, "he (Peter) commanded them to be baptized in the name of the Lord". (verse 48)

My friend, now that you have accepted Jesus as your friend and Master, please write me a little note, so that I may rejoice with you.

Here is my name and address:

Gus Lenis,
6249 Marine Avenue,
Powell River, B.C.,
Canada, V8A 4K6

# BIBLIOGRAPHY

In the Bible quotations used, I took the liberty to insert italics, to place words in parenthesis and to use different fonts, in an attempt to emphasize -- not to alter the Scriptures.

Being Greek, I chose to do my research from the original Greek. Most of my quotations came from:

THE  INTERLINEAR BIBLE (HEBREW, GREEK, ENGLISH)
BY JAY P. GREEN, SR.

I also used :

ZONDERVAN'S INTERLINEAR
(GREEK---ENGLISH) NEW TESTAMENT

The SEPTUAGINT WITH APOCRYPHA:
GREEK AND ENGLISH
(SIR LANCELOT C. T. BRENTON)

ROTHERHAM EMPHASIZED BIBLE

NESTLE-ALAND
NOVUM TESTAMENTUM GRAECE

THE KING JAMES BIBLE

NEW INTERNATIONAL VERSION (NIV)

NEW WORLD TRANSLATION (NWT)
OF JEHOVAH' S WITNESSES

Other books I used were :

IGNATIUS' LETTERS TO EPHESIANS, ROMANS, SMYRNAEANS

IRENAEUS -- AGAINST HERESIES

ATHENAGORAS -- A PLEA REGARDING CHRISTIANS

POLYCARP -- MARTYRDOM OF POLYCARP

JUSTIN -- DIALOGUE WITH TRYPHO THE JEW

DIVRYS GREEK / ENGLISH DICTIONARY, 1971

ORTHOGRAPHICON ERMINEYTIKON "1970" NEON LEXICON
(DIMITRAKOY)

STRONG'S EXHAUSTIVE CONCORDANCE OF THE BIBLE

WEBSTER'S NEW WORLD DICTIONARY "1966"

JEHOVAH'S WITNESSES' PUBLICATION
"SHOULD YOU BELIEVE IN THE TRINITY?
- Is Jesus Christ the Almighty God?"

CRUEL AND ANUSUAL PUNISHMENT
DUANE MAGNANI

JEHOVAH'S WITNESSES, JESUS CHRIST,
AND THE GOSPEL OF JOHN
ROBERT M. BOWMAN, JR.

# SCRIPTURE INDEX

# APPENDIX A

## Scriptures which prove that the prehuman Jesus was MICHAEL THE ARCHANGEL

Listed on this page is every known scripture which proves that Jesus, in His prehuman life, was Michael the Archangel as taught by the Jehovah's Witnesses:

# APPENDIX B

## ONE OF THE SERIOUS ERRORS OF THE NEW WORLD TRANSLATION

Men who present themselves as true Christians, have deliberately changed the words of the Bible in order to try to deceive and to mislead those who are searching for the true nature of our Lord Jesus Christ.

Whether they know it or not, they are assisting Satan in his quest to blind men from seeing the divine glory of our Lord.

When they produced their "New World Translation" of the Bible, they changed and twisted almost every scripture which reveals the divine glory of Jesus. In fact, in certain places, they did not even translate from the original Greek --- they inserted their false doctrine and presented it as being part of the written word of God. For instance, in John 1:4, the apostle John, writing in Greek wrote about Jesus:

"ΕΝ    ΑΥΤΩ    ΖΩΗ    ΗΝ"
In     Him     life     was

The word "ΕΝ" in Greek is a preposition and it means "in" --- not "in union with" as the Jehovah's Witnesses often translate it. The Greek grammar dictates that when "ΕΝ" is followed by a word which is in the dative case, it means: within, inside. (Check ΛΕΞΙΚΟΝ ΔΗΜΗΤΡΑΚΟΥ, Page 528.)

180.

"AYTΩ" means "Him", and it is in the dative case!

"EN AYTΩ" means "in (within) Him".

"ZΩH" means "life".

"HN" means "was".

"EN AYTΩ ZΩH HN" means "in (within) Him life was", or "in Him was life".

The above four words show that life was inside Jesus. This idea corresponds with other scriptures which plainly state that Jesus is "the life". (John 11:25; 1 John 1:2). Only God is the life, therefore, Jesus is God.

In the New World Translation of the Bible, the translators present John 1:4 as follows:

*"What has come into existence by means of him was life"!*

From the above, we observe that out of the four words, "in Him was life", only the last three words have been correctly translated from the Greek. What happened to the first word "in"?

First, it has disappeared !

Second, it has been replaced with a long phrase which now reads "What has come into existence by means of" ! !

The above phrase is not the translation of the Greek word "EN"--- which means only "IN".

What the JW's are obviously trying to do is to obscure the meaning and importance of the idea that LIFE WAS IN JESUS ! Why are they doing this? Because they do not want to admit that Jesus is God.

Should we say that they have made an innocent grammatical error? I don't think that they are so innocent or ignorant ! In their zeal to strip Jesus of His Godly glory, they have deliberately altered the wording and meaning of the Scriptures. I'm sure that Satan is pleased with their work.

May God YHWH rebuke them. One day, they will stand before the "living Word of God" and they will have to give an account to Him for trying to degrade and belittle Him (Hebr. 4:12, 13). But, until that day comes, you do not have to follow them. You do not have to believe in a lie. You do not have to preach their deceptions from door to door. Be like the Beroeans and check carefully from the Scriptures the things they try to teach you. The Bible says that the Beroeans ". . . searched the scriptures daily, whether those things were so." (Acts 17:11)

# APPENDIX C

## ΑΡΧΗ  (pronounced Arche)

When the Greek word "ΑΡΧΗ" is used to indicate place or time of starting of an event, it means "beginning", e.g. "In the beginning (ΑΡΧΗ) was the Word . . ." (John 1:1). However, when it refers to a person, it means: Author(-ity), Government, Power, Cause, First Cause. For instance, in Luke 20:20 we read, ". . . so as to deliver Him (Jesus) to the power (ΑΡΧΗ) and the authority of the governor." Here, the word ΑΡΧΗ has been translated correctly as "power" --- not "beginning". The word "beginning" would not have made any sense in this sentence. Also check: Luke 12:11; Romans 8:38; 1 Cor. 15:24; Eph. 1:21; 3:10; 6:12; Col. 1:16; 2:10, 15; Tit. 3:1.

In Revelation 3:14, we read: ". . . These things saith the Amen . . . the beginning of the creation of God". In the Greek text, the phrase "the beginning of the creation of God" appears as follows:

| "Η | ΑΡΧΗ | ΤΗΣ | ΚΤΙΣΕΩΣ | ΤΟΥ | ΘΕΟΥ" |
|------|------------|--------|----------|--------|------|
| the | "beginning"? | of the | creation | of the | God |

In the above phrase the word "ΑΡΧΗ" refers to the person "Amen". Therefore, as it does not indicate time or place, it does not mean "beginning"; it means "Author" or "Power". The translators of the NIV, and the Interlinear Bible --- by Jay P. Green, Sr., have recognized this, and have translated it as follows:

". . . the ruler of God's creation." (NIV)

". . . the Head of the creation of God."
(The Interlinear Bible)


    In translating the above phrase, other
translators of the Bible incorrectly used the
word "beginning" for the Greek word "ΑΡΧΗ".
By doing so, however, they have left the doors
open to certain people who believe that Jesus is a
created being. For instance, the Jehovah's
Witnesses preach that the expression "the
beginning of the creation of God", actually
means that Jesus is "the first creature which God
created" !

    To those who believe that this is what the
Greek text says, I emphatically say that they are
wrong. If the apostle John, who wrote the book
of Revelation, wanted to indicate that Jesus is
"the first creature which God created", he would
have had to use the Greek word "ΑΠΑΡΧΗ". In
this case, the above phrase would appear in the
Greek as "Η ΑΠΑΡΧΗ ΤΗΣ ΚΤΙΣΕΩΣ ΤΟΥ ΘΕΟΥ".
    The word "ΑΠΑΡΧΗ" means: *"the first and
the best out of a group of people or things"*. There
is no direct English word to correspond to the
Greek word "ΑΠΑΡΧΗ". The Bible translators
have translated this word as "firstfruits".
Therefore, if John had used the word "ΑΠΑΡΧΗ",
this sentence would have appeared in English as
"the firstfruits of the creation of God"! But such
is not the case!
    The word "ΑΠΑΡΧΗ" (firstfruits) appears in

the following scriptures:

"But Christ has indeed been raised from the dead, the firstfruits (ΑΠΑΡΧΗ) of those who have fallen asleep." (1 Cor. 15:20)

"But each in his own turn; Christ, the firstfruits (ΑΠΑΡΧΗ); then, when He comes, those who belong to Him." (1 Cor. 15:23)

Other scriptures where the word "ΑΠΑΡΧΗ" appears, in the Greek text, are: Romans 8:23; 11:16; 16:5; 1 Cor. 16:15; 2 Thes. 2:13; James 1:18; Rev. 14:4.

From the above study, we see that Revelation 3:14 <u>does not say</u> Jesus is the first created being which God created. Instead, it says Jesus is the Author, the Leader, or the Power which created all God's creation. Therefore, the Greek phrase "Η ΑΡΧΗ ΤΗΣ ΚΤΙΣΕΩΣ ΤΟΥ ΘΕΟΥ", should have been translated as:

# "the Author (or the Power) of the creation of God".

This corresponds with John 1:3 where it says, "through him* all things were made; without him nothing was made that has been made." (NIV)

---

* About the expression "through him", please read pages 124 to 127 of this book.

# APPENDIX D

## THE GREEK ARTICLE "THE", ITS FORMS & USAGE

In the Greek language all the nouns have a gender; they appear either as masculine, feminine, or neuter. e.g. "the word" (Ο ΛΟΓΟΣ) is masculine, "the door" (Η ΘΥΡΑ) is feminine, and "the water" (ΤΟ ΥΔΩΡ) is neuter.

In the Greek, the article "the" also has different genders in order to co-ordinate with the gender of the noun to which it refers. The article "the" appears in its three genders as Ο, Η, ΤΟ. "Ο" for masculine; "Η" for feminine; and "ΤΟ" for neuter.

The form of the article "the" (Ο, Η, ΤΟ) also changes depending on whether the noun to which it refers is found in the singular or plural form, and whether it is in the nominative, genitive, dative, accusative, or the vocative case. Here, I list all its different forms:

| CASE | SINGULAR | | | PLURAL | | |
|------|------|------|------|------|------|------|
| | MAS. | FEM. | NEUT. | MAS. | FEM. | NEUT. |
| NOM. | Ο | Η | ΤΟ | ΟΙ | ΑΙ | ΤΑ |
| GEN. | ΤΟΥ | ΤΗΣ | ΤΟΥ | ΤΩΝ | ΤΩΝ | ΤΩΝ |
| DAT. | ΤΩ | ΤΗ | ΤΩ | ΤΟΙΣ | ΤΑΙΣ | ΤΟΙΣ |
| ACC. | ΤΟΝ | ΤΗΝ | ΤΟ | ΤΟΥΣ | ΤΑΣ | ΤΑ |
| VOC. | Ω | Ω | Ω | Ω | Ω | Ω |

In a sentence, we may have the subject, the linking verb, and a subjective complement or predicate. The subject is a word or a group of words about which something is said, while the predicate makes a statement about the subject.

When one constructs a sentence in English or Greek, one usually places the subject before the linking verb while the predicate is placed after it. In Greek, the predicate may appear in the beginning, in the middle, or at the end of a sentence. Usually, <u>when the predicate appears after the linking verb, the predicate noun takes the article, and when it appears before the linking verb, it does not.</u> The reason for this is so that the predicate will not be confused with the subject.

The above rule was explained by E. C. Colwell and was published in the <u>Journal of Biblical Literature</u> in 1933, with the title, "A Definite Rule for the Use of the Article in the Greek New Testament." He wrote:

"A definite predicate nominative has the article when it follows the verb; it does not have the article when it precedes the verb."

Towards the end of his essay he concluded: "The following rules may be tentatively formulated to describe the use of the article with definite predicate nouns in sentences in which the verb occurs. (1) Definite predicate nouns here regularly take the article. (2) The exceptions are for the most part due to a change in word-order: (a) Definite predicate nouns which follow the verb (this is the usual order) usually take the article; (b) Definite predicate nouns which precede the verb usually lack the article (c) Proper names regularly lack the article in the predicate;

(d) Predicate nominatives in relative clauses regularly follow the verb whether or not they have the article."

Colwell's study has been accepted as a genuine contribution to the field of Greek biblical scholarship. The following is the statement of L.C. McGaughy from his 1970 doctoral dissertation (completed under Robert W. Funk, one of America's foremost Greek grammarians, whose dissertation was on the Greek article):

"In a pioneer study of 1933, E.C. Colwell has conclusively demonstrated that such speculative statements [as that nouns with the article are definite while those without the article are indefinite, or that the use or nonuse of the article indicates various theological nuances, or that the fluctuation is merely stylistic], which are mainly based on private hunches, need not serve as the basis for a grammar of the article with predicates of S-II sentences [i.e., sentences with a subject noun, a linking verb, and a "subjective complement" or predicate nominative] stands as a model of descriptive analysis for New Testament Greek studies."

(For more details, read the book, Jehovah's Witnesses, Jesus Christ, and the Gospel of John, by Robert M. Bowman, Jr.).

In John 1:1, there are three small sentences or clauses:

a)    EN    APXH    HN    O    ΛΟΓΟΣ
      In    beginning   was    the    Word

b)  O    ΛΟΓΟΣ    HN    ΠΡΟΣ   TON    ΘΕΟΝ
    the    Word     was    with    the     God


c)    ΘΕΟΣ    HN    O    ΛΟΓΟΣ
      God     was    the   Word


Now, let us examine clauses b)  and c) :

clause (b)

"O    ΛΟΓΟΣ | HN | ΠΡΟΣ   TON    ΘΕΟΝ"
the    Word   | was |  with    the     God

The word-order here follows the usual sentence construction. The subject "O    ΛΟΓΟΣ" (the Word) holds the first position, followed by the linking verb "HN" (was), which is followed by the predicate "ΠΡΟΣ TON    ΘΕΟΝ" (with the God). Therefore, the predicate noun "ΘΕΟΝ" (God) has retained its article "TON" (the).

clause (c).

"ΘΕΟΣ | HN | O    ΛΟΓΟΣ"
God   | was | the   Word

In this clause, the subject is again "O ΛΟΓΟΣ" (the Word). The linking verb is "HN" (was). The predicate is the noun "ΘΕΟΣ" (God). What we notice here is that the predicate noun (God) is placed before the linking verb (was) and therefore, it does not retain its article.

To add the article "a" in front of the predicate noun "ΘΕΟΣ" (God) is incorrect. To translate clause c as "and the Word was a god", as the Witnesses have done, is misleading, is an error, and constitutes a heresy.

If John had wanted to state that the Word was "a god", another god, as the Witnesses teach, he would have written clause c as follows:

"ΚΑΙ     ΘΕΟΣ     ΤΙΣ     ΗΝ     Ο     ΛΟΓΟΣ"
and       God       a       was     the     Word.

But this is <u>not</u> the case. John did <u>not</u> write it that way. Instead, he wrote:

"ΘΕΟΣ     ΗΝ     Ο     ΛΟΓΟΣ"
God      was     the     Word

The above must be translated into English as:

"the Word was God".

This sentence does not mean that the Word was "the God" (the Father) with whom the Word was from the beginning as stated in John 1:1,2. Clause c) states one thing only --- that the Word, the pre-human Jesus, was God by nature. To put it another way, it means that the essence of the "Word" is exactly the same as the Father's.

The absence of the article "the" from before a predicate noun (whether that noun is qualititative, adjectival, definite or indefinite) does not change or weaken the basic meaning of that noun. Thus, the Jehovah's Witnesses do not have any valid grammatical rule on which to base their decision to add the article "a" in front of the word "God" --- none at all!   If their only excuse for adding the article "a" is the absence of the article "the" before the word "ΘΕΟΣ" (God), then I challenge them to be consistent and do the same in the following verses where the article "the" is not found before the word "God" in the original Greek text: Matthew 5:9; 6:24; Luke 1:35; 2:40; John 1:6; Phil. 1:11. Then, according to their NWT, these scriptures would read:

Matthew 5:9  "Happy are the peaceable, for they will be called 'sons of <u>a god</u>'."

Luke 1:35  "In answer the angel said to her: "Holy spirit will come upon you, and power of the Most High will overshadow you. For that reason also what is born will be called holy, <u>a god's Son.</u>"

Luke 2:40   "And the young child continued growing and getting strong, being filled with wisdom, and <u>a god's</u> favor continued upon him."

John 1:6   "There arose a man that was sent forth as a representative of <u>a god</u>; his name was John."

Phillippians 1:11   "and may be filled with righteous fruit, which is through Jesus Christ, to <u>a god's</u> glory and praise."

Such statements would be very misleading.

# APPENDIX E

Listed here are a few false prophecies given by the Jehovah's Witnesses:

**A.)** In 1889, the Witnesses prophesied that the battle of Armagedon will end in A.D. 1914.
**"The Kingdom of God is already begun, in A.D. 1878, and that the "battle of the great day of God Almighty" (Rev. 16:14), which will end in A.D. 1914 with the complete overthrow of earth's present rulership, is already commenced."**
**(The Time is at Hand, 1889, p.101)**

**B.)** They also prophesied that Christ will overthrow the nations before 1914 A.D. and that His Kingdom will be fully established in that year.
"In the preceding chapter we presented evidence showing that the "Times of the Gentiles" or **their lease of dominion will run fully out with the year A.D. 1914, and that at that time, they will all be overturned and Christ's Kingdom fully established.** That the Lord must be present, and set up his Kingdom, and exercise his great power so as to dash the nations to pieces as a potter's vessel, is then clearly fixed; for it is "in the days of these kings" --- **before their overthrow (i.e. before A.D. 1914) that the God of Heaven will set up his Kingdom."**
**(The Time is at Hand, 1889, p.170)**

**C.)** In 1921 and 1922, they prophesied that Abraham, Isaak, Jacob and other faithful ones would be resurrected in the year 1925.

**192.**

"The chief thing to be restored is the human race to life; and since other Scriptures definitely fix the fact that there will be a resurrection of Abraham, Isaak, Jacob and other faithful ones of old, and that these will have the first favor, **we may expect 1925 to witness the return of these faithful men of Israel from the condition of death,** being resurrected and fully restored to perfect humanity and made the visible, legal representatives of the new order of things on earth, right here in Jerusalem."

**(The Golden Age, 3/18/21, p.381, under the subtitle "The Jubilee", para. 3)**

". . . Lo, our King is here, **and the year 1925 marks the date when all shall see His mighty power demonstrated in the resurrection of the ancient worthies, and the time when 'millions now living will never die'. "**
**(The Golden Age, 3/1/22, p.350, para. 1)**

**D.)** Later, they prophesied that the dissolving of the kingdoms (Satan's empire), will be completed by the year 1925 A.D.

**"The dissolving of Satan's empire began in the World War; and there is no possible restoration of any crumbling kingdom, but rather the crushing, disintegrating process continues until all shall cease to function. The Scriptures seem to limit this transition period to eleven years, from 1914 to and including 1925."**
**(The Golden Age, 6/6/23, p.563)**

With the following comments, the false prophets of the Watchtower Society also manipulated their followers and made them believe that the "sabbatic" thousand year reign of Jesus Christ would begin in 1975 A.D.

". . . According to this trustworthy Bible chronology **six thousand years from man's creation, will end in 1975, and the seventh period of a thousand years of human history will begin in the fall of 1975 C.E. . . . How appropriate it would be for Jehovah God to make of this coming seventh period of a thousand years a sabbath period of rest and release, a great jubilee sabbath for the proclaiming of liberty throughout the earth to all its inhabitants ! This would be most timely for mankind.** It would also be most fitting on God's part, for, remember, mankind has yet ahead of it what the last book of the Holy Bible speaks of as the reign of Jesus Christ over earth for a thousand years, the millennial reign of Christ. . . . **It would not be by mere chance or accident but would be according to the loving purpose of Jehovah God for the reign of Jesus Christ, the 'Lord of the sabbath,' to run parallel with the seventh millenium of man's existence...** there is now every reason why the human creation will yet be set free, not by men, but by Almighty God. **The long-awaited time for this is at hand !"**
(**Life Everlasting --- in Freedom of the Sons of God**, 1966, pp. 29-30)

". . . He predicted that **by 1975** this world would be too dangerous ! . . . **this date is also the one indicated by the most reliable Bible research as marking the end of 6,000 years of rebellion of men and demons against God."**
**(**AWAKE!**, 1/8/68, p.19)**

"More recently, earnest researchers of the Holy Bible have made a recheck of its chronology. According to their calculations the six millenniums of mankind's life on earth **would end in the mid-seventies. Thus the seventh millennium from man's creation by Jehovah God would begin within less than ten years.**

**In order for the Lord Jesus Christ to be** "Lord even of the sabbath day,"**his thousand-year reign would have to be the seventh in a series of thousand-year periods or millenniums. Thus it would be a sabbatic reign . . . Would not, then, the end of six millenniums** of mankind's laborious enslavement under Satan the Devil **be the fitting time for Jehovah God to usher in a Sabbath mill-ennium for all his human creatures? Yes, indeed !**

**And his King Jesus Christ will be Lord of that Sabbath."**
**(**THE WATCHTOWER**, 10/5/69, pp. 622, 623, 39, 42)**